of the world-famous maestro, and it also animates him as a man of his time—a loving husband and an adoring father to the daughter who writes insightfully and lovingly about the career in which [Samuel Antek] was poised to achieve even greater heights."

—Sybil Steinberg, Contributing Editor and Former
Book Review Editor for *Publishers Weekly*

"[Samuel Antek's] lucid description of Toscanini in rehearsal is the best account I have ever read of what it is like to create music at the highest level of intensity. He makes us feel we are with the musicians, both cowering in fear of another angry explosion and playing their hearts out for the man whose approval they so desperately wanted. Lucy Antek Johnson . . . has provided valuable context and brings alive an era when classical music rang out from Studio 8H at 30 Rock."

—Orin Grossman, Pianist and Lecturer

"Of the many books about Toscanini, perhaps the closest portrait of playing with the maestro was violinist and conductor Samuel Antek's, which accompanied Robert Hupka's legendary photos. In this new edition, Lucy Antek Johnson has given us the story behind *This Was Toscanini*, filled with new details of the man who so keenly observed the great conductor's genius and humility, told from the point of view of a loving daughter."

—Jay Shulman, Cellist

"One shares the experience of being under Toscanini's baton . . . it is as though one were in the maestro's living presence."

—*Kirkus Reviews* (1963)

This Was
TOSCANINI

The Maestro, My Father, and Me

This Was TOSCANINI

The Maestro, My Father, and Me

New & Expanded Edition

Samuel Antek

Lucy Antek Johnson

BROWN BOOKS
PUBLISHING GROUP

This Was Toscanini
The Maestro, My Father, and Me

Brown Books Publishing Group
Dallas / New York
www.BrownBooks.com
(972) 381-0009

A New Era in Publishing®

Publisher's Cataloging-In-Publication Data

Names: Antek, Samuel, author. | Johnson, Lucy Antek, 1946- author.
Title: This was Toscanini : the maestro, my father, and me / Samuel
    Antek, Lucy Antek Johnson.
Description: New & expanded edition. | Dallas ; New York : Brown
    Books Publishing Group, [2021]
Identifiers: ISBN 9781612545202
Subjects: LCSH: Toscanini, Arturo, 1867-1957--Influence. | Antek,
    Samuel. | Conductors (Music)--United States--Biography.
    | Concertmasters--United States--Biography. | Fathers and
    daughters. | LCGFT: Biographies.
Classification: LCC ML422.T67 A75 2021 | DDC 784.2092--dc23

ISBN 978-1-61254-520-2
LCCN 2021901892

Printed in China
10 9 8 7 6 5 4 3 2 1

For more information or to contact the author, please
go to www.LucyAntekJohnson.com.

For my darling husband, Bill, and . . .

To the immortal memories of Arturo Toscanini
and Alice and Sam Antek.

*"Non voglio più sentire le note, non ci devono essere
più note . . .*

        Abbandonatevi al Vostro cuore."

        —Arturo Toscanini

*"I don't want to hear notes anymore, there shouldn't
be any more notes . . .*

        Abandon yourself to your heart."

CONTENTS

Foreword xv

Prelude xxi

PLAYING WITH TOSCANINI

Introduction 1

Chapter One 5

TOURING WITH TOSCANINI

Introduction 45

Chapter Two 55

RECORDING WITH TOSCANINI

Introduction 67

Chapter Three 73

A VISIT WITH TOSCANINI

Introduction 83

Chapter Four 91

TOSCANINI CONDUCTS OBERON

Introduction 109

Chapter Five 113

Coda 155

Acknowledgments 163

Photo Credits 167

About the Authors 169

FOREWORD

Harvey Sachs

MORE THAN SIXTY YEARS after his death, Arturo Toscanini remains a gigantic figure in the world of classical music. He was one of the most intelligent, profound, scrupulous, and dynamic performing musicians in history, as well as the first conductor to have left recordings of a very large portion of his repertoire. His work as an interpreter was so original and so powerful that it has influenced musicians down to our own day. Generations of conductors—even those who disagreed or disagree with his performances or recordings—have been the beneficiaries of his reforms in the opera house and concert hall. His insistence that the performer's job is to come as close as possible to revealing the composer's intentions, rather than to use the music as a vehicle for self-expression, remains a golden rule for many of today's outstanding conductors, instrumentalists, and singers. In addition, the intransigent personality that allowed him to accomplish his reforms and pursue his musical ideals also led him to stand up to Europe's fascist regimes in the 1930s. As a result, he became an example of nonpartisan political morality.

Toscanini was born in Parma in 1867 into a lower-middle-class artisan family. By the time he graduated at eighteen from Parma's conservatory, his passion for music, his great talents—including a photographic memory—and his high standards regarding musical performance were fully developed. The following year, while serving as principal cellist and assistant chorus master in a touring Italian opera company in Brazil, he was suddenly called upon to replace the ensemble's regular conductor. He then took over the rest of the tour, rehearsing and performing all twelve operas from memory.

The young Maestro developed his skills in the major and minor opera houses of his native country. At twenty-five, he conducted the world premiere of Leoncavallo's *Pagliacci*. Three years later, he became principal conductor of Turin's Teatro Regio, where he led, among many other works, the world premiere of Puccini's *La bohème*, the first Italian production of Wagner's *Götterdämmerung*, and the national and/or local premieres of more than fifty symphonic works. A little later, during his first seven seasons as La Scala's principal conductor, Toscanini gave the Italian premieres of Wagner's *Siegfried*, Tchaikovsky's *Eugene Onegin*, Richard Strauss's *Salome*, Debussy's *Pelléas et Mélisande*, and orchestral works by many important contemporary composers. At the Metropolitan Opera (1908–15), Toscanini's enormous workload included the world premiere of Puccini's *La fanciulla del West* and the American premiere of Mussorgsky's *Boris Godunov*. During the 1920s, when he commanded the Scala ensemble in what was probably the most glorious period in the house's history, he led the world premiere of *Turandot*, Puccini's last opera, which was also the last Italian opera to enter the internationally popular repertoire.

Toscanini conducted the New York Philharmonic from 1926 to 1936, and in 1930 he became the first non-German-school conductor to perform at the Bayreuth Festival, where he was hailed by the Wagner family and others as the greatest interpreter of that composer's music. But he withdrew from Bayreuth upon Hitler's accession to power in Germany. In Italy, he had been opposed to Mussolini's regime since its inception in 1922, and in Bologna in 1931 he was physically attacked by fascists for refusing to conduct their party's hymn. He then vowed not to work in Italy unless the regime fell—and, in fact, he did not conduct there again until after World War II. He performed at the Salzburg Festival from 1934 until Austria's "Nazification" in 1938, after which he cofounded Switzerland's Lucerne Festival as an alternative venue. In an act of solidarity with refugee European Jewish musicians, he traveled to Palestine twice at his own expense in the 1930s to conduct what later became the Israel Philharmonic Orchestra.

Over the years, he also performed in most major European capitals, as well as in many parts of North and South America. His repertoire included approximately 120 operas and well over 400 symphonic works—all rehearsed and performed from memory.

In 1937, at the age of seventy, Toscanini assumed direction of the NBC Symphony Orchestra in New York (newly created for him), where, for the following seventeen years, he conducted hundreds of radio broadcasts and recordings and ten groundbreaking telecasts. During World War II, he helped to raise money for the Allies and the Red Cross, and he aided refugee musicians from Europe. He retired in 1954, at the age of eighty-seven, and died in New York in 1957, a few weeks before his ninetieth birthday.

This is the bare-bones outline of Arturo Toscanini's remarkable life and career. To get to the essence of who he was, however, we in the twenty-first century must listen to his recordings and read whatever firsthand accounts we can find about him and his work.

There are three major English-language sources of information about Toscanini the musician, all written from the point of view of musicians who worked with him. The earliest of these is the chapter dedicated to Toscanini in *The Orchestra Speaks* (1938) by Bernard Shore, who was the principal viola of the BBC Symphony Orchestra during the years 1935–39, when Toscanini worked frequently with that ensemble. The latest was B. H. Haggin's *The Toscanini Musicians Knew* (1967, expanded and reprinted in 1989 as part of *Arturo Toscanini: Contemporary Recollections of the Maestro*, edited by Thomas Hathaway). But between those two volumes came the most interesting of all: *This Was Toscanini* (1963) by Samuel Antek, a member of Toscanini's NBC Symphony Orchestra during the entire seventeen years of its existence. It was Antek's book, with its beautiful photos by Robert Hupka, that we young (at the time!) Toscanini admirers found to be the most thorough, the most substantial, the best organized, and the liveliest of them all.

All three of these volumes have long been out of print, but Lucy Antek Johnson, Samuel Antek's daughter, has undertaken—as a true labor of love—the task of reissuing her father's text and making it available to twenty-first-century readers well over half a century after its initial publication. She has taken advantage not only of her father's original words and of many of Robert Hupka's original photos but also of her father's letters and other writings, her mother's notes, and her own memories as a child growing up at a time when Toscanini and his NBC Symphony were a mainstay of orchestral music in North America and beyond. In her commentary, she conveys the full flavor of those years and that particular milieu. She brings her gifted father back to life for us, just as his words brought Toscanini back to life.

Anyone interested not only in Toscanini but in orchestral life in mid-twentieth-century America will treasure this book.

Harvey Sachs, whose biography *Toscanini: Musician of Conscience* was published to international critical acclaim in 2017, is the author or coauthor of ten books and has written for the *New Yorker*, the *New York Times*, the *Times Literary Supplement*, and many other publications. He lives in New York and is on the faculty of the Curtis Institute of Music in Philadelphia.

PRELUDE

Lucy Antek Johnson

MY FATHER, SAMUEL ANTEK, was only twenty-nine years old when he was handpicked to be a first violinist in the NBC Symphony, an orchestra especially created for Arturo Toscanini, regarded as the greatest conductor of his time. Tens of thousands of Toscanini enthusiasts clamored for tickets to his performances, filling arenas around the world. He was, by modern standards, a rock star.

Dad was a member of this prestigious orchestra from its debut performance on the NBC Radio Network—Christmas night, 1937—to the final broadcast in April of 1954, when Toscanini retired at the age of eighty-seven.

This Was Toscanini is not a biography. It is my father's musical memoir, an intimate behind-the-scenes portrait of the Maestro and of his orchestra told from the unique perspective of a musician fortunate enough to play under Toscanini's legendary leadership in hundreds of concerts, almost a thousand rehearsals, and innumerable recording sessions.

My father brings alive the work that made those memorable concerts possible, sharing stories about the Maestro's particular approach to a score, his conducting style, and, of course, his infamous moods. As he says in the handwritten notes he sent to his publisher: "I will describe what I have actually seen, felt, and heard Toscanini say. What he asked of us, those who made music with him."

First published in 1963, my father's book remains the most comprehensive personal narrative about working with the Maestro. It is a story about the passion and dedication it takes to make great music and about Toscanini's singular and often volatile approach to music making. It is also a story about the formation of a new orchestra under the baton of a musical genius who not only was a force throughout his twentieth-century career but who possessed an artistry and style that resonate even now, more than sixty-five years after his last concert.

In 2017, the 150th anniversary of Toscanini's birth, articles about the Maestro examined and praised his impact on classical music. In that same year, Harvey Sachs's biography *Toscanini: Musician of Conscience* was published to international acclaim. Sachs presented new personal material about the Maestro and, to my delight, quoted passages from my father's book. I was proud to see that Dad's writing was still relevant, even though his book had been out of print for more than thirty-five years.

Sachs's biography inspired me to reread *This Was Toscanini*. An elegant marriage of narrative and photographs, the book has been prominently displayed wherever I have lived, but I had not read it straight through since its original publication many decades before.

On a gray winter afternoon, I settled into my favorite chair, overlooking trees heavy with snow. I took a sip of mint tea and began to read. Within minutes, I was captivated, drawn into the power of Toscanini's personality, the artistry of Robert Hupka's iconic photographs, and the eloquence and charm of my father's words. As music critic and novelist Marcia Davenport noted in her foreword to the original publication, "Mr. Antek could write as well as he played . . . truthful, moving, and intensely alive."

When I finally looked up from the book, it was evening. Along with the joy of feeling so close to my dad, I experienced a familiar sadness—he was not here to share in the moment. I couldn't turn to him and say, "Bravo!"

Rereading my father's book convinced me that it deserved a renewed life. It was time to introduce his work to new generations of musicians, students, and classical music fans. My reading also inspired me to bring my father's own story into the spotlight. Who was Samuel Antek? In this book, he tells about his years with the Maestro, but he reveals little about himself. What were *his* dreams? *His* choices? *His* challenges?

As a child prodigy, soloist, member of a famed orchestra, and successful conductor in his own right, my father also had a story to tell. It is now my turn to tell it, as well as to share my impressions of what it was like to grow up with such a dynamic father in a home where Toscanini made so great an impact.

In order to tell my father's story—and our story—I needed to answer some questions for myself. Those early years had become a foggy mix of memory and family lore. How old was Dad when he first picked up a violin? How did working with Toscanini influence his career decisions? When did I realize that my dad wasn't like my friends' dads? They worked in offices during the day. He worked in a concert hall at night.

Where would I look for the answers? I had already outlived my parents and had no friends or family of their generation to turn to. I decided to begin with the boxes of memorabilia that had been stored in my basement for years, each with "Toscanini" or "Sam" scrawled across the top. These boxes had traveled with me from home to home, from one side of the country to the other. I had looked through these cherished keepsakes before, but never with such a specific mission. Now I carefully sifted through the stacks of old photographs, yellowing journals, notated musical scores, fragile news clippings and reviews, letters, and scratchy recordings. I also spent hours at the New York Public Library for the Performing Arts, poring over my father's papers in the archive I had donated to the library in 2006.

Every photo evoked a long-forgotten story or a vivid personal memory. Reading Dad's many interviews, I could almost hear his voice, with its faint echo of a Chicago accent. When I stared at candid shots of him coming offstage, still beaming with a postperformance glow, I easily summoned up his engaging laugh and broad smile. My time immersed in these treasures touched me deeply. Each reminiscence, each insight, each revelation helped bring my father's story and his legacy into focus. I was ready to plunge in and go wherever this journey took me.

But how to organize all this material? The task seemed daunting. I was a television producer, not a researcher. Yet I had spent my entire career working with writers,

hundreds of them, nurturing their ideas, helping them to shape and reshape their scripts and shepherding their stories from the first creative spark to the finished product. It was time to apply my forty years of experience to my own labor of love.

Music was my father's profession, but it was also a family activity. My mother, Alice, a professional artist and illustrator, was also an amateur pianist. She could play any song by ear and become the life of the party as she deftly switched gears from a Beethoven sonata to the latest Rodgers and Hammerstein show tune. She frequently accompanied my father at their impromptu Sunday musicales.

As for me, it was never a question of *if* I would study an instrument; rather, the question was which one. At a very young age, I sat at the piano, barely reaching the keyboard, plunking out notes with my plump little fingers. By the time I was six, it was settled—piano was to be the instrument of choice. I began taking lessons and eventually worked my way up from the simple "Here We Go, Up a Row," a beginner's piece of three notes for only three fingers, to the more complex and classic "Minuet in G" by Bach using both hands.

These days, whenever I get the urge to sit down to play, which sadly is not very often, I turn to the same few pieces that I conquered many years ago. With a little bit of practice, I can still do justice to a Chopin prelude.

In the 1940s, my father pursued his dream to conduct—a dream he had been cultivating since his student years. With the support and encouragement of the Maestro, Dad launched his own career as a conductor. While continuing to play first violin for NBC, he was appointed musical director of the New Jersey Symphony in 1947 and was invited to guest conduct major orchestras around the country. When Toscanini offered him the precious opportunity to guest conduct the NBC Symphony, my father's future as a conductor was sealed.

In 1950, his heightened recognition both as a conductor and as a violinist under Toscanini's direction led the *Saturday Review*, a distinguished literary magazine, to commission him to write about his experience of working with the Maestro. His article

"Playing with the Maestro" was so well received that Toscanini was heard to say, "He wrote very beautiful about me. Very *simpatico*." High praise, indeed. Dad was soon approached by a publisher to expand his story into a book—this book.

For the next few years, in addition to the increased demands of his schedule and the surge of celebrity that went along with it, he filled reams of lined yellow pads and wore out boxes of number 2 pencils creating his manuscript. When he wasn't sitting at the piano meticulously reviewing a thick orchestral score for an upcoming concert with the New Jersey Symphony, or selecting a program for a children's concert with the Philadelphia Orchestra, or practicing his violin for an NBC performance, he wrote. My mother dutifully typed up each draft, tapping away on her trusty Royal manual typewriter, while I, wanting to get into the act, helped her proofread the pages. Dad, his sweet-smelling pipe smoke wafting through the apartment, wrote, rewrote, and rewrote again late into the night.

Tragically, my father didn't live to write the final chapter. He collapsed and died of a heart attack on January 27, 1958. He was only forty-nine. I was only twelve. That Monday morning, I left for school, waving goodbye to him as he ate his usual quartered orange and toasted english muffin, and by the afternoon, he was gone. It was that sudden.

This Was Toscanini was published posthumously five years later. My father never got to read the remarkable reviews or receive the overwhelming praise from his friends and colleagues—praise he would have treasured.

I'm honored to return my father to center stage to tell his story about the Maestro who made such a dazzling impression on him, on the audience, and on the other players of the NBC Symphony Orchestra. I introduce each of the book's original chapters with reflections of my own, creating a richer portrait of Samuel Antek, our life together, and the illustrious era in which he flourished as a musician.

To Jamuel Antek
Cordial remembrance of
(March 25-1945) Arturo Toscanini

Introduction
PLAYING WITH TOSCANINI

ALTHOUGH I WASN'T EVEN born when the NBC Symphony was created and have only a dim memory of ever meeting the Maestro, I do recall that Arturo Toscanini was always a central figure in our home. His autographed portrait sat atop our Steinway Grand, the gleaming ebony piano that stood majestically in the living room of our Upper West Side apartment in New York City. That photograph still occupies a place of honor today atop the same piano, now in my Connecticut living room.

Toscanini's NBC Symphony radio concerts were broadcast live on Saturday nights from Studio 8H, a concert hall built within the NBC studios at 30 Rockefeller Plaza. Millions of music lovers all over the world tuned in each week.

Those Saturday evenings were special events in our house. I remember my father, in all his six-foot-two splendor, spiffed up in his formal evening clothes, his violin case tucked under his arm, waiting patiently at the front door for my mother before they headed downtown for the performance. Soon my mother would glide down the hall, her floor-length teal-blue taffeta skirt rustling as she walked. She would stand at the long hall mirror, put on her signature hat and veil, pick up her evening gloves, then tilt her head to the right, making sure everything was in its proper place. Once the door closed behind them, her floral scent hung in the air, a lingering hint of their glamorous night ahead.

I was much too young to attend the concerts, but I was allowed to stay up late and listen to the broadcasts. My aunt, my cousin Toby, and I would sit on the sofa facing the mahogany console that housed the bulky radio. As soon as we heard Ben Grauer—the official voice of the NBC Symphony—make his opening announcement, I lit up with excitement, ready for the concert to start. The studio audience exploded into applause at Toscanini's entrance, then abruptly hushed in the slight pause before his downbeat. Once the orchestra started to play, I truly believed I could hear the particular sound of my daddy's violin.

At breakfast the next morning, I listened quietly as my parents discussed the concert. Didn't the Beethoven tempo seem a bit too fast? Why had Toscanini tensed up during the performance? Hadn't he seemed more relaxed at the rehearsal? (Not always, I was soon to learn. Toscanini was, in fact, renowned for his grueling rehearsal sessions.)

After one of those challenging rehearsal days, my parents' conversation around the dinner table inevitably turned to the "Old Man," the affectionate term the players called their revered Maestro. I would soak up stories about Toscanini's exacting musical demands or about one of his unpredictable flare-ups of temper—neither of which dampened the players' spirits but rather inspired them to strive even harder as artists.

What was their first rehearsal like? That moment of meeting the legendary Maestro? They had practiced and performed for weeks with other conductors—including Pierre Monteux and Artur Rodziński—in preparation for this day. Samuel Antek and his fellow musicians were nervous as they waited for Toscanini to arrive. They were about to begin the first rehearsal for their premiere performance under the baton of one of the most famous men in the world. They were about to make musical history.

Let's let my father tell the story.

THE NATIONAL BROADCASTING COMPANY

Presents

ARTURO TOSCANINI

Conducting

THE NBC SYMPHONY ORCHESTRA

CHRISTMAS NIGHT

Saturday, December 25, 1937

10:00 TO 11:30 P.M., EST.

in NBC Studio 8-H—Radio City

Program

Concerto Grosso in D Minor, Opus 3, No. 11 . . . . *Vivaldi*

Symphony in G Minor . . . . *Mozart*

Symphony No. 1, in C Minor . . . . *Brahms*

———

These programs are broadcast over the
combined NBC Blue and Red Networks.

*Since the modern microphone is extremely sensitive, your co-operation
in maintaining strict silence during the music is urgently requested.*

———

PROGRAM FOR NEW YEAR'S NIGHT

JANUARY 1, 1938

Symphony in C Major . . . . *Schubert*

Two Movements from String Quartet in F Major, Opus 135 . . . *Beethoven*
  (a) Lento Assai, Cantante e tranquillo
  (b) Vivace

"Death and Transfiguration" . . . . *Richard Strauss*

*Programs were printed on silk, cork, and cardboard, instead of paper, so that no rustling
sounds would be picked up by the audience microphones during a "live" broadcast.*

Chapter One
PLAYING WITH TOSCANINI

IN THE FALL OF 1937, a great symphony orchestra, brought together from the far corners of the world, sat in rapt and tingling silence on the huge stage of Studio 8H in Radio City, New York. I was a violinist in that orchestra, and we were awaiting the first appearance of our conductor. There was no audience. The men, instruments in hand, sat nervously rigid, scarcely breathing. Suddenly, from a door on the right side of the stage, a small, solidly built man emerged. Immediately discernible were the crowning white hair and the impassive, square, high-cheek boned, bemustached face. He was dressed in a severely cut black alpaca jacket, with a high clerical collar, formal striped trousers, and pointed, slipper-like shoes. In his hand he carried a baton. In awed stillness, we watched covertly as he walked up the few steps leading to the stage.

As he stepped up to the podium, we all rose, like puppets suddenly propelled to life by the pent-up tension. We had been warned in advance not to make any vocal demonstration, and we stood silent, eagerly and anxiously staring.

He looked around, apparently bewildered by our unexpected action, and gestured a faint greeting with both arms, a mechanical smile lighting his pale face for an instant. Somewhat embarrassed, we sat down again. Then, in a rough, hoarse voice, he called out, "Brahms!" He looked at us piercingly for the briefest moment, then raised his arms. In one smashing stroke, the baton came down. A vibrant sound suddenly gushed forth from the tense players.

Thus began my first rehearsal with Arturo Toscanini—his first with the newly formed NBC Symphony. He, who was to become our beloved "Old Man," was then seventy.

With each heart-pounding timpani stroke in the opening bars of Brahms's First Symphony, his baton beat became more powerful, more insistent, his shoulders strained and hunched as though buffeting a giant wind. His outstretched left arm spasmodically flailed the air, the cupped fingers pleading like a beseeching beggar. His face reddened, muscles tightened, eyes and eyebrows constantly moving.

As we in the violin section tore with our bows against our strings, I felt I was being sucked into a roaring maelstrom of sound—every bit of strength and skill called upon and strained into being. Bits of breath, muscle, and blood never before used were being drained from me. I sensed, more than I heard, with near disbelief, the new sounds around me. Was this the same music we had been practicing so assiduously for days? Like ships torn from their mooring in a stormy ocean, we bobbed and tossed, responding to these earnest, importuning gestures. With what a new fierce joy we played!

"So! So! So!" he bellowed. *Cantare! Sostenere!* His legs were bending slightly as he braced himself for his violent movements, which were becoming larger, more pile driving, as the music reached its first great climax. *Cantare! Sostenere!* I was to hear these words often in the years to come. "Sing! Sustain!" Toscanini's battle cry! This was the first time they were flung at us, and for seventeen years we lived by them.

Toscanini often said, "Any *asino* can conduct—but to make music . . . eh? Is *difficile!*" Playing with Toscanini was a musical rebirth. The clarity, intensity, and honesty of his musical vision—his own torment—was like a cleansing baptismal pool. Caught up in his force, your own indifference was washed away. You were not just a player, another musician, but an artist once more searching for long-forgotten ideals and truths. You were curiously alive, and there was purpose and self-fulfillment in your work. It was not a job; it was a calling.

Like every great leader, Toscanini never demanded anything of his orchestra beyond what he himself had already given in full measure. "Look at me! I give everything— *everything!*" he would scream hoarsely, beating his chest with his clenched fist. "*Look at me! VERGOGNA!* Shame on you—*you*—YOU!"

Toscanini not only lived music; he, more than any musician I have ever known, made music seem like life itself. In his struggle for ultimate truth, Toscanini never gave up. He was always St. George fighting the dragon that was guarding the musical treasure. And to me, it was tremendously exciting and a privilege to be caught up in this great battle with him.

I shall always remember the rehearsal in October 1938 the morning Germany marched into the Sudetenland. In the streets, people crowded around radios and newspaper stands, waiting for the latest word. The musicians of the NBC Symphony were gathered in the dressing room downstairs, arguing and debating while the air was electric with impending catastrophe. As the time for rehearsal drew near, we sluggishly, almost resentfully, began to make our way upstairs. How unimportant the rehearsal seemed that morning. Armies were poised for combat. What was a mere rehearsal at a time like this? How impatient and indifferent the men were, anxious to get back into the reality of the world. And then the small figure appeared. With beetled brows, downcast face, Toscanini stepped up to the podium. He looked around at us for a moment, waved his arms briefly; then: "Good morning. Beethoven!"

No sooner had the orchestra begun to play than it seemed mesmerized, the outside world, with its tragedy, forgotten. "Play! Don't sleep! Is a crescendo! Is a *sforzando!* Put something! You do nothing! You want to go sleep? Go home! Move the bow! *Arco! Arco!*" he screamed. We were all caught up in the passion of the moment. Beethoven became the battlefield, as important as any in the world. Each accent, each crackling crescendo came to life, to full triumphant meaning. This was no moth-eaten masterpiece; this was searing human truth and reality. We were playing Beethoven with Toscanini, reveling in creation and proud of our talent. This was our reason for being.

Such a man was Toscanini. No conductor I ever worked with could create quite this feeling of ecstasy. What a sense of excitement and discovery each rehearsal brought as we watched and heard Toscanini find, in an old familiar work, a note, an accent, a nuance hitherto completely unnoticed or glossed over by routine or carelessness. Under his baton, time-wearied, shopworn pieces regained their original luster and shone anew—freshly minted coins. "*La routine*—the death of music!" Toscanini would wail. "What is routine but the last bad performance!"

We marveled at the extraordinary gifts of this great musician: his fabulous ear, his unbelievable sense of musical proportion and discipline, his incredible memory, his driving stamina. Every day, as we played with him, we were dazzled and confounded by his almost superhuman qualities.

Toscanini had attained a pinnacle of honor and success matched by few persons of any age, but despite this, he seemed an unhappy man. While his unique gifts illuminated all that could possibly be brought to light, in working with him we always sensed his frustration in reaching for something—a beauty, an understanding—just beyond his grasp. We sensed his despair and his uncertainty, and we loved him for it.

Experimenting was one of his outstanding qualities. Even in his eighties, he seemed curiously adolescent. When he would change a tempo or phrase, he would insist on it with wrathful conviction; but the following day, smiling rather sheepishly, he would change it again. "You know, sometimes I am stupid too—no?"

Every detail, every bit of ornamentation, every grace note or pizzicato throbbed within him. "Nobody can hear it—never! *Nobody!*" he would cry, gesturing to the empty theater. In something as seemingly innocent as the Air in Bach's Orchestral Suite no. 3, he clucked over each trill and turn like a fretful hen. I remember, as I passed his room before one concert, he was hunched over the piano, trying different ornamentations for the last bar. Then, just as we were going on, word came of a change from the final rehearsal.

One of his most violent displays of temper concerned nothing more than two grace notes that had not been articulated in Wagner's *Tannhäuser* Overture, a momentous crime in Toscanini's eyes. "The small notes! The small notes!" he would shout. These seeming minutiae were terribly important to him. And they became so to us, because to Toscanini music was no game of wits or cerebral discourse, no set of studied postures and words. It was no mere titillation of the ear, no mere gratification of the senses, no intellectual ash heap for musicologists and academicians. It was dramatically personal and elemental. It was also sheer physical struggle, and he was fearful to behold as he roared his defiance at the devils that were preventing *his* pianissimo from coming into being, *his* rubato from falling into place, *his* tempo from pulsing forth. Every movement of his baton, every motion of his hands, even every burst of rage served music.

I have seen him rip his jacket to shreds in exasperation because he felt the orchestra was holding back in its attention and zeal. Dramatic? Stagy? Theatrical? Yes! But always so wonderfully honest, sincere, and so extraordinarily effective in creating

the mood and feeling within us that he sought. His hoarse, frenzied, bawling of "*Vergogna!* (Shame!)" would balefully rend the air, or the menacing "*Corpo del vostro Dio!*" Sometimes, in a mounting wave of petulant chagrin and anger, his voice would grow more vitriolic and irascible, until the words seemed to rack his throat. "*No!* You play a *pasticcio!*" he would scream—a mess. "Speak clear! *Non mangiare le note!* (Don't eat the notes!) You eat the note!" Then, suddenly relenting, his face would light up with an unexpected smile and he would say, "Yes, it is a *pasticcio*, it is difficult, no?" Earnestly and naïvely, like a child, he would go on. "Is difficult for me too, no? Now we wash, we clean the passage. *Santo Dio*, we try, yes?" A resounding smack of the baton on the score, and we would try. And if it didn't go, there he was, demoniacal again. That sweat-drenched face was bearing down upon us like the archangel of vengeance himself as we almost disemboweled ourselves with feverish effort. Then, suddenly, a spine-chilling wail: "Pi-a-a-a-n-o-o! Bassi! Contrabassi! You grunt away like pigs! You sound as if you were scratching your bellies—szshrump! Szshrump!" he would bellow while tearing at his clothes, viciously pantomiming the scratching. "*Corpo del vostro Dio!* PI-A-ANO!"

"But Maestro," a player would sometimes protest in a small, hesitant, and resentful voice. "My part is printed 'forte.'"

"What you say?" the Old Man would growl menacingly, unbelievingly, distracted for the moment from his tirade.

"It says 'forte,'" the player would reply, this time in an even smaller, more apologetic voice.

"What? Forte? *Forte?*" with an air of incredulity. "What means 'forte'? *Ignorante!* Is a stupid word—as stupid as you! Is a thousand fortes—all kinds of fortes. Sometimes forte is pia-a-a-no, piano is forte! *Accidenti!* (Damn it!) You call yourself a musician? *O, per Dio santissimo!* You play here in THIS orchestra? In a village café house you belong! You don't listen to what others play. Your nose in the music—szshrump! Szshrump! You hear nothing! You cover up the oboe solo! One poor oboe—one!—and you szshrump!

Szshrump! Where are your ears? Look at me! *Contra-ba-a-ss-i!*" in a long, drawn-out wail. *"Tutti! Tutti! Vergogna!"*

The whole episode would have ended much sooner had the player not spoken up, for you never could wring any satisfaction from the Old Man. He was never at a loss for words or the energy to throw them at you—and always with that peculiar musical logic that seemed to justify his opinions.

Then he would continue, his eyes staring as though at an apparition, arms outstretched, pleading—and your heart would melt with affection and tenderness.

I have often heard it said, almost in parrot fashion, that Toscanini was a "perfectionist," an opinion that has always irritated me. Toscanini, I felt, never sought perfection—he sought music. Music was life; does one expect life to be perfect? Toscanini's music making always had a craggy and elemental quality. In his insistence on *vita* (life), our playing was often rougher than it was with most other conductors.

Toscanini would never demean himself or insult us by making things easier through mere "safe" conducting "technique." There was a musical mood or truth to be grappled with that was more important. *"Corpo del vostro Dio!"* he would cry. "Are you men or babies?" Did we have to be suckled? "Eat, baby, *eat!*" With irascible irony, he would make the motions of giving us his breast like a nursing mother. "Eat, babies—shame on *you! Ignoranti!*"

During the many years I played with Toscanini, he never sat down at a rehearsal. On the podium there was never the usual high-legged stool that many conductors use. I have seen him standing, bathed in perspiration, through rehearsals lasting hours, conducting with the greatest intensity, driving himself and exhausting us. Once, at a particular point during an especially long rehearsal—longer than I ever heard of with any other conductor—his legs were so stiffened from standing in one position, he could hardly move. He stared at the floor and, with a breathless, tired, whooshing sigh of relief, plopped down, spent and forlorn, on the podium.

There was always a furious pride in Toscanini. "If I am tired or sick," he once said to me, "I don't come at all! I sleep home. As long as I am here, I stand and conduct. I don't sleep!"

In all the years I played with him, he never missed a rehearsal or a performance.

I cannot recall his ever making a gesture that was purely mechanical, impersonal, and not closely identified in mood or movement with the expression of the musical phrase as he felt it. He conducted the music, not the orchestra. This he did with extreme simplicity and without ostentatious display or physical mannerisms. Toscanini's conducting was the most controlled and self-disciplined of any conductor with whom I have ever worked. He never struck a consciously dramatic pose or allowed himself a moment of narcissistic posturing. His movements were usually confined to the space directly before him and almost entirely between the shoulder and the waist. With legs slightly apart and seldom changing their position, he always seemed to bend slightly forward from the waist, particularly in the softer or more tender passages. You felt it brought him into more intimate contact with the playing, not unlike someone hovering over or shielding a delicate flame.

He always held the baton with his full hand around the stick, the blunt end fitting firmly against the lower palm of his hand, with thumb, second, and third fingers extending almost straight and unbending to support it, fourth and fifth fingers curled gracefully, like a polite tea drinker.

In soft, singing passages, he kept his arm extended before him, partially crooked at the elbow, with baton almost parallel to his chest. The undulating movements were always essentially "arm" movements, masculine and virile. I never saw him conduct with wrist or finger movements of his right hand. To him, these picayune gestures were out of keeping with the dignity and nobility of his music making. No matter how intimate or delicate the playing, his movements always conveyed a feeling of the music's breadth

and substance. His left arm was almost always extended, too, the hand open, weaving closely along as though ready to catch hold should something happen. Pianissimos were always indicated, of course, by the smallness of his baton beat and the slight flickering of the fingers of his left hand. At rehearsals, in particularly soft sections, he often cried in an agonized voice, "Far away—far away. . ." For a very hushed effect, he brought the tip of the index finger of his left hand to his lips as though saying, "Sh! Sh!"

For even greater expressiveness, he brought his left hand over his heart and indicated an undulating motion, as though playing a wide cello vibrato. "Play with your hearts, not your instruments!"

When the music was dramatic and vehemently rhythmic, Toscanini's beats did not become longer; they became, instead, shorter. As he moved to the climactic moment of the work, Toscanini's chin sank to his chest, his shoulders hunched, his face became choleric. Now the baton, usually pointed up for the more serene melodic passages, faced toward the ground.

Every ounce of pile-driving force and intensity seemed to be concentrated in each stroke. The beckoning left arm became like a flailing beater, shaking loose every bit of sound you could produce. You felt with him as he seemed to strain every muscle to burst the chains shackling his arms.

"The bow! *Dio santo!*" he would bellow. "Use the bow!" Everyone bobbed frantically and swayed with each bow stroke. The storm and fury of sound, suddenly released, burst forth with almost unbelievable intensity and sonority.

It is interesting, however, to note that it was we, the players, who did all the bobbing and weaving; Toscanini, in spite of the intensity and fury, did not move from his spot. There was no wild fanning of the air, and yet you felt his complete, passionate involvement in the music. Few conductors have the power to evoke so deep a musical response from an orchestra. This was one of Toscanini's unique abilities.

Although Toscanini was noted as the world's greatest conductor, his baton "technique," from a technical standpoint, was far from exceptional. When I toured the United States with the NBC Symphony, I invariably met musicians and writers in all parts of the country who would question me about this seeming paradox. How could the world's greatest conductor not be an exceptional "conductor"? This seemed to confuse many people who thought of a conductor essentially in relation to stick-waving mechanics. The answer is, of course, that Toscanini never concerned himself much with the mechanics of stick beating. He was primarily interested in the musical problem and its solution. He was not too concerned with helping the orchestra mechanically, and I always felt that he himself did not know quite what he was doing with his baton. Toscanini was not a studied conductor but an intuitive one and often spoke rather contemptuously of those who studied or taught conducting per se. If there was a choice to be made between conducting in a way that would make it easy for the orchestra to play together or conducting in a way that would hold together the musical line, he would always choose the latter and castigate the men in the orchestra for not doing the mechanics themselves. "Is difficult for me too!" he would cry out as he persisted in conducting a 3/2 bar in "two" and insisted that the orchestra make the complicated division for itself.

A fine example of this is the slow movement of Debussy's *Ibéria*. Over the many years I played it with him, both in the studio and on tour, this particular section had never been satisfactorily or clearly performed. Always, in spite of innumerable rehearsals, we would find ourselves "swimming," the section's complexities being such that Toscanini's feeling of the flow of the music somehow always left us adrift without our knowing where, exactly, the beat was. Many batons were broken, stands demolished, and poor musicians excoriated into numb despair because Toscanini felt it had to be conducted exactly *that* way—his way—in spite of anything or everything that happened. The confusion persisted to the very last time I played it with him, when we recorded *Ibéria* a few days after we had returned from our national tour. Once more, at the same place, the orchestra seemed to fall apart. Again Toscanini screamed. Again the curses were hurled. And finally he cried, "Don't look at the stupid stick in my hand! I don't know myself what it does. But feel—feel what I want. Try to understand!" I remember that, with great

concentrated effort, the passage came through, finally, wonderfully free in the rubato and expressive in color. But I knew if we should ever play it again, the battle would have to be fought all over. All the confusion and anxiety could have been easily resolved had he conducted this passage with mechanical precision, as every other conductor does. But his fierce pride resisted such a solution. I felt he would rather die than conduct mechanically for ensemble reasons, in order to obtain what he felt should be achieved by the men.

There are many instances of this kind of stubborn adherence to a musical conviction. In slow pieces, such as the prelude to Wagner's *Parsifal* or the opening of Strauss's *Death and Transfiguration*, Toscanini would give only the broadest indication of the tempo and no more. He insisted that the men themselves make the subdivision into eighths, sixteenths, or triplets. Often, these plans did not work, and he would almost unconsciously start to subdivide when the ensemble began to fall apart. But when the orchestra did achieve the desired self-control and elasticity, the spaciousness and nobility of the musical utterances were tremendously evocative and moving. The music seemed to flow completely from the organic musical center and impulse of the orchestra itself.

Another very expressive gesture in Toscanini's conducting occurred when the music became particularly poignant and intense with inner feeling, such as at the end of the Funeral March of Beethoven's *Eroica*. He would crouch slightly, lean a little more toward us, indicating with his baton the merest suggestion of a still, precise, flowing beat. His left hand was brought almost to the side of his face, his curled fingers moved spasmodically, as though fingering each note we were playing. "Weeping . . . weeping!" he would cry out in a high, choked wail. The few bars of soli for the first violins toward the end of the slow movement of the *Eroica* were gone over time and time again whenever we played it. In a hoarse, tear-drenched, bleating voice, he would sing it over for us, conducting as he sang. The most important thing in the world was that *that* expression be given. "Put something!" he would implore, motioning to his heart. We would play it through. "*Non c'e male* (not bad)," he would say, "but the tone—so *brutto* (ugly). Find the tone—the sound—you have the right one in your instrument. Find it—down on the fingerboard— f-a-a-r away . . . f-a-a-r away . . . in the sky . . . suffering! . . . s-u-u-ffering!"

Toscanini never spoke matter of factly. Excitement and dramatic expressiveness filled his improvised word clusters. I could feel each member of the orchestra straining every ounce of his imagination and technique to attain the sound and mood Toscanini wanted. The sound that finally emerged differed as completely from what we had originally played as does refined gold from the original ore. We would nod to one another, beaming with satisfaction and almost disbelief at the transformation.

We were continually exhorted to "sing," not to "play," and to sustain each note for its fullest value in melodic phrases. "*Sostenere*," he would say as he waved his arms before him in slow, pendulum-like movements. Toscanini would resort to this gesture in music of broad melodic warmth. "Look at me! Look at my stick!" he would call out to a player. "See what I do!"—making that slow, swinging motion. "*So!*—not *so*, like you!"—making an impersonal mechanical beat. "*No, no—tenere!* Long note! Hold the notes! *Non solfeggiato!* SING!"

These were demands peculiarly typical of Toscanini. What he wanted was not only that each note of a melody come on its appointed beat but that the note be evenly spread and sustained over the full value of the beat. The effect would be almost like moving in slow motion from one note to another rather than hopping quickly from note to note. It meant holding on to each note as long as possible before moving to the next. This gave an unusually broad, flowing, gliding quality to a succession of notes. A quarter note did not seem to be just one quarter or even two eighth notes. It was as though you felt that one beat was sixteen sixty-fourth notes, each of equal importance; in other words, each quarter note had to be spread evenly over one complete beat of time. Each note then seemed more significant, full blown, richer, and sustained into the note that followed it.

To achieve this kind of playing consumed a great deal of rehearsal time, for Toscanini, more than any other conductor, would stop at individual soli in the various instruments to insist upon this sustained expressiveness, which gave particular weight and consequence to a melody and to its personalized sound. As usual, Toscanini would sing it: "So-o-o!" Then again: "Put some blood in each note! You have water in your veins! Feel something! This is music, not notes. *Corpo del vostro Dio! Tenere, tenere*; sing—not nyah-nyah-nyah!" Here he would venomously ridicule the playing by making peevish sounds like a whining child. "No, *no! Cantare! Cantare!* Look at me! Watch my stupid stick! It is more intelligent than you! *ANCORA!* Be intelligent! Be quick to understand! *VERGOGNA!*"

Another typical conducting gesture was a circular beat, like a penmanship writing exercise. This was sometimes used in a boisterous rhythmic section, such as is found in a Rossini overture. It seemed to give momentum and continuous sweep. Instead of beating the quarters of a 4/4, 2/4, or 3/4 tempo in the conventional bar patterns, he gave each beat a circular shape and continued it without indicating the bar lines.

With Toscanini, giving entrance cues to the various instruments or choirs always seemed incidental. Since his attention usually focused on clarity, musical line, and mood, those men waiting for cues were often left to fend for themselves. Nor would he interrupt the flow of his beat to give an obvious cue. A whole bass and cello section would come crashing in with no more than a quick sharp glance from him as preparation. Many conductors make cue-giving the occasion for violent and dramatic display and gesture. Some, in their concern about the entrance of a player or of a whole section, unhappily break contact with the mood and flow of the music and continually flick indications with their baton or left hand. They often impress the players in this way with their knowledge of the intricacies of the score, sometimes indulging in exaggerated movements that have no relationship either to the continuity of the music or to its feeling. Toscanini's complete self-effacement—his never seeking to intrude himself between the music and the listener in order to display his knowledge or to capture the limelight as he stood before the audience—was indeed a rare quality among conductors. His was a form of modesty, a sense of propriety, and a reverence for his art that made him especially loved and respected by us. An orchestra is quick to sense and resent blatant showmanship or insincerity on the part of a conductor, and while players often have to tolerate this, it sometimes tends to make them quite indifferent in their playing and causes them to hold back that indefinable something of their own creativity.

As a conductor, however, there were really two Toscaninis: the conductor at rehearsals and the conductor at concerts. And they were quite different.

At concerts, Toscanini was invariably tense and controlled, becoming an aristocrat rather than the peasant he had been at rehearsals. This transformation always affected the orchestra's performance. Sensing his tension, the men themselves became tense and nervous and often could not give their utmost. Our best fights were often left at rehearsals, like those of a prizefighter's left in the gym. Sometimes the men were quite disconsolate after a performance, great as it might have seemed to the public. "Too bad!" we'd say as we trooped to our dressing room. "Hope the Old Man isn't too upset!"

At rehearsal, Toscanini was much more relaxed, and as a result, his gestures were much less inhibited. They were more florid, more free, and more expressive. The very fact that he could shout, bellow, and sing apparently freed him physically. At concerts, he seemed to freeze; his movements were smaller, less emotional, more restrained. I often had the impression, watching him during a performance, that he almost wished he were invisible so as not to come between the audience and the music. His formality and seeming remoteness were in direct contrast to the behavior of almost all other conductors, who usually save themselves for the concert. It was almost as though he were saying, "We have rehearsed. You know what we worked out; you are artists, not children. I don't have to stand before you and make stupid gestures. You understand. You feel the music we have rehearsed." I felt as though he wanted to be there merely as a reminder of what had been worked out during rehearsals. Toscanini seemed to sense the awkwardness, even the absurdity, of gesticulating in public by waving a "stupid"

stick as though he were actually producing the sounds. After all, it was *we* who were doing the playing.

Toscanini never smiled at a concert. There was never a personal or friendly reassuring glance or movement from him. He seemed deadly serious, and that seriousness was communicated to the orchestra. I have often felt the pity of it—that those wonderfully evocative performances at rehearsals, the real Toscanini, as it were, were so seldom heard.

But Toscanini could not always maintain this restraint at concerts. Sometimes, if a particular passage fell apart, he would sadly and despairingly shake his head as if saying, "Well, we failed!" At other times, if a player or a section did something especially displeasing, his head would rock balefully, as though to say, "Wait . . . wait till I get my hands on you!" And if a player made a wrong entrance or played indifferently (at least in Toscanini's opinion!), Toscanini would actually shake a clenched fist at the hapless victim, and his face would grow stony with rage. While his right hand carried on with the conducting almost mechanically, he would spit out some of his choice epithets through clenched teeth.

On tour, however, the atmosphere was completely different. For this reason, I look back on our concerts on the road with particular sentiment and relish, for I believe they were the finest we ever gave. It was not the stimulation of huge audiences and strange cities but rather the difference in the Old Man himself. He would smile, almost chuckle, at the tumultuous reception of the audiences. The whole orchestra was conscious of the difference in him, of a wonderful balance between tension and relaxed concentration, and as a result, the men gave of themselves more freely. At last, on tour, I had the satisfying feeling that a concert was really as good as a rehearsal!

Sitting on the stage in our Studio 8H at NBC with Toscanini often reminded me of sitting in the sanctuary of a church, of participating in a solemn spiritual rite rather than performing at a concert. Coming from Toscanini, even oaths and curses seemed almost devout. I felt as if each note we played had a profound religious significance, and his exhortation of "Put blood!" always made me conscious of the trial and agony of artistic creation, of the effort involved in the sheer writing of every one of the myriad notes in a composition, as if the composer's pen had been dipped in his blood, not in ink. Under Toscanini, each note, each detail, each nuance seemed epic.

One of my earliest and strongest impressions when I first played with Toscanini was that of the earthy, emotional reality he gave to music. Music seemed part of everyday living and feeling. It never seemed abstract. Under him, the life and death, the poetry and beauty of Beethoven, for example, became peculiarly real. An accent or sforzando was a stab of physical pain; a poignant or tragic musical phrase was as dire and personal as a dreaded war communiqué; a little dynamic inflection was a tender caress. No matter how monumental the canvas of a composition, no matter how old or new the music—whether classic, romantic, or modern—under Toscanini's direction it immediately became part of your very breathing. How did he do it? I believe his musicians became fascinated, almost hypnotized, by Toscanini's complete and utter absorption, by his tremendous involvement in the projection of the music. By word, by gesture, by song, by rages, he conjured up the mood and picture he felt. So vividly, colorfully, and dramatically was this done that we grasped completely what he sought to convey. "More crescendo!"—"Less crescendo!"—"More bow!"—"Less bow!"—more this—less that. But beyond these demands was his emotional aura, in which we were all enveloped. He might bellow, rage, plead, but always with such touching sincerity. The image he created became not only clear to us but peculiarly and convincingly our own. We did not feel like puppets being made or told to do something; we felt completely identified with what was going on. Music was no longer abstract notes; it was the symbol of our most moving, deeply felt experience.

A phrase such as the opening of Beethoven's Sixth Symphony was gone over time and time again whenever we rehearsed it. I remember once spending about half an hour on just the opening bars. No other conductor would prod and probe further and deeper beyond the façade of musical notation to discover its innermost meaning. I shall always treasure as one of my most beautiful memories the picture of Toscanini singing the *Pastorale*'s opening phrase: a man transfigured—his face uplifted, his arms and hands so gracefully and tenderly pantomiming the theme. When we played, I felt as if I were playing alone—as if mine were the responsibility of achieving this inexpressible atmosphere of benediction. How we worked for the relationship of the slurred notes and the separated notes to be made without accent and self-consciousness, with just that right quality of floating sound—the slight ritard at the end of the first phrase—like a gentle sigh running its limpid course effortlessly and inevitably to the fermata.

All these details were worked over again and again. And then the "bahlance," as Toscanini would say. No other musician or conductor had his acute sense of proportion between the various strands of sound played by different instruments in the orchestra. Unerringly, he would single out exactly the note that had to be strengthened or diminished to fit the well-balanced whole. Four instruments playing a chord would be so beautifully blended and fused that they would sound as one.

I should speak at this point of another Toscanini phenomenon that made working with him so much more meaningful and inspiring than listening to and watching him conduct from the audience. I shall try to put my finger on something very obscure and formless, but something that might possibly throw further light on the inexplicable magnetism Toscanini exerted on the musicians. Just as one's instrument has a vibration and sensation never felt by the listener, so, too, is it with the players of the orchestra. We ourselves, personally, emotionally, along with our instruments, are the vibrating "instruments" upon which a conductor plays—we feel and sense things that no listener can ever quite approximate.

A reader may say, "That's all very fine and very interesting, but results are what count. How does it sound?" For the listener, this is the important question, whether it be a

Toscanini performance or that of any other conductor with an orchestra. On this basis, no future musical historian will be able to evaluate properly Toscanini's greatness. His greatness is attested to not so much by his performances but by the tremendous power and incandescence he inspired in his "instrument"—the orchestra—and the hold he had over those who played with him. His greatness is attested to by the unimpeachable honesty and integrity, the warm humanity that showed forth most brilliantly in his working process. It lay in what he felt rather than in what was finally heard by the listener. The sounds we made meant one thing to a listener; to us, making those same sounds, there was an intangibly added reverberation and sensitivity no instrument could mechanically measure, unless it were possible somehow to calculate electronically the warm pulsating bond that flowed between Toscanini and his musicians. The results in sound alone will always, to me, seem almost sterile and commonplace in comparison. It was this spiritual, unseen, but deeply felt relationship that truly expressed and meant "Toscanini" to us. It was a feeling born of inspired sympathy and understanding—of working together toward goals and ideals often long forgotten on our parts but so greatly appreciated and so spiritually sustaining.

It is these feelings that we who played with him treasured so deeply. It is the radiance lighted in us, rather than the music that was only heard by others, that remains the distilled essence of the effectiveness of a Toscanini. Only we, the vibrating instruments, could perhaps truly grasp and understand why Toscanini was "just different."

It was an arresting experience to sit on the stage facing him. His face was broad and muscular, its bone structure bold. Standing on the podium, he seemed almost tall. But I was somewhat surprised every time I spoke to him to realize how small he actually was. The most outstanding feature of his unusually handsome face was his eyes, which had a strange and enigmatic expression. Toscanini was, of course, very nearsighted, but in spite of this, on the podium, he never wore his glasses. When he had occasion to refer to the score, he brought it up to within an inch of his face, as though smelling it, or bent down to the music on the stand. But though he seemingly had poor vision, he could

spot the slightest bow movement of a bass player thirty feet away or the movement of a violinist at the back of the orchestra. The actual expression on his face closely resembled that of a blind person; his eyes had that vacant, staring quality of somehow not being focused. When he addressed himself to a section of the orchestra, he seemed to be looking through it, not at it. At times this puzzled the players, particularly when he lashed out at one of them with a venomous comment. We were never quite sure at whom he was looking, for his unfocused, angry stare seemed to be accusing us all. He reminded me of one of those heroic sculptures by Michelangelo in which the faces are shown in all their strength and spiritual devotion but the eyes are left vacant. Not that Toscanini's eyes were expressionless. Deep-set, under bristling gray eyebrows, they blazed with excitement and spiritual light, even though they always seemed to be looking through and beyond rather than at you.

When he was actually conducting, Toscanini's face was one of the most expressive I have ever seen. And yet, paradoxically, it did not mirror the passing moods of the music as an actor's might; it was completely free of that kind of conscious histrionic display. Only the clenched teeth, taut face and neck muscles, flushed skin, perspiration, and the wide-open staring eyes conveyed the feeling of his total and passionate involvement. When, in moments of great tenderness in the music, his half-closed eyes seemed to peer into the distance, I was fascinated by the players' reaction, the hush, the eerie quiet that enveloped us.

In talking to musicians, orchestral players, and soloists—or in reading about their musical reactions and experiences—you will find that they single out playing with Toscanini as the crowning point of their careers. Of even greater significance, I think, is the peculiar warmth that comes to a musician's voice and the glow that lights up his face when he talks about Toscanini, a reaction I very keenly sense in myself. Musicians speak of Toscanini's dramatic outbursts, his rages, his feats of memory, his amazing ear, and many other aspects of his musical genius. However, just as the greater part of an iceberg is hidden from view, so, too, beneath the wonder and stimulation of Toscanini's great gifts lay subtle, indefinable qualities, submerged but even more meaningful.

The musicians who make up our larger orchestras are a mixed group with varied personalities, backgrounds, and skills. They may be divided most simply into two groups: the wind players and the string players. In training, achievement, and musical outlook, these two groups differ greatly. Everyone who studies a wind instrument professionally accepts the fact that he or she will end up playing in an orchestra. String players are different. To the string player, a symphony orchestra offers little opportunity for personal expression or individual artistic creativity. As their original enthusiasms become dull and jaded, music making itself becomes a monotonous grind and playing in a symphony orchestra but another way of making a living, one far removed from the dreams and desires that prompted the grueling work required to master an instrument.

What has all this to do with Toscanini? Toscanini, like great leaders in other fields, had the gift of sweeping away the cobwebs of lost faiths, of dulled sensitivities. When you played with him, you felt you were once more an individual, an artist, not a nonentity. This made you bring to everything you did, every note you played, the same intensity and expressiveness you sought when playing alone. You were once more stimulated, challenged to give your best. Music making became once more a hallowed calling and you felt musically reborn. *You loved music again.*

We played to please the Old Man, but our own taste buds of artistic awareness were sharpened, and we were inspired to play and satisfy our own highest standards and instincts in pursuit of our common goal. The terrors and abuses Toscanini hurled at us were accepted and tolerated because they sprang from his own humility, sincerity, and love for the music. Every giant artist drives himself as much. We were completely won over and carried along with Toscanini's musical approach, its unerring, never-exaggerated good taste. The performance was *ours*, not only Toscanini's, for he was but the voice of our own musical consciences. *We were playing with Toscanini! We were musicians!*

No conductor more grudgingly accepted recognition from audience and orchestra alike for his achievement. On the other hand, to no other conductor did the orchestra more willingly and gratefully pass on the credit and acclaim for a performance. The actual playing was, of course, ours, but we were so caught up in the Old Man's striving, in his dynamism, that we always spoke of how *he* "played" it. Many times, at rehearsals, players would spontaneously break into applause when a particular phrase would shine with unusual luster. Toscanini never acknowledged these compliments. "*No!* Is not me!" he would say almost angrily. "Is in the music, just before your eyes. But you don't see— *look to the score! Look to the notes! Don't play from memory!* Oh!" he would say, making an anguished gesture of supplication, hands raised, and face to the ceiling. "*La routine!*

The routine! The curse of music! *Study* your part—I always look to my score no matter how many times I play! *Corpo del vostro Dio! Vergogna!*" Sometimes he accented these tirades by slamming his hand so violently on the music that it would almost seem to break his arms. At other times, somewhat humorously, in a particularly good mood, he would pat himself on the cheek, saying with an air of resignation, *"Bravo*, Toscanini! *Vergogna YOU! Pazienza*, Toscanini! *Pazienza! You* are a *stupido! I*"—patting his chest— "am intelligent."

To be intelligent, to be an honest man, were the greatest compliments I ever heard Toscanini pay a fellow musician. By "intelligence" he meant the capacity to understand, to grasp quickly, to sense the qualities he himself would try to express by combinations of pantomime and song. Even when he informally discussed the playing of various members of the orchestra, off the podium I never heard him say someone played beautifully. He would talk about the beautiful music, but if he wanted to compliment the player, he would merely say, *"Bene*—he is *molto intelligente." "Non c'e male!* (Not so bad!)" and *"Bene!* (Good!)" were the highest praise indeed. The most exquisite playing was accepted with little comment, as if such playing were expected. That was why we were there—what other way was there to play?

An incident concerning the late Guido Cantelli, the outstanding young Italian who was with us as guest conductor, revealed more than anything else Toscanini's peculiar feeling about praising an orchestra. Cantelli had done a program of modern works with us, a program of unusual difficulty, which the orchestra had performed with great virtuosity and brilliance. At the first rehearsal after the concert, Cantelli tried to express his thanks to the orchestra for their marvelous cooperation and skill. He told us that when he had played these works in Europe with other orchestras, they had required many more rehearsals. He interrupted his little speech suddenly to say, "You know, I was talking to the Maestro yesterday. He heard the performance, too, and liked it. I told him how thrilled I was with your performance and what a wonderful orchestra you are. Maestro stopped me and said, 'Yes, is true—but whatever you do, never say *bravo* to the orchestra. Don't tell them!' But"—Cantelli smiled and went on—"I can't help it. I must say *bravo, bravo!*" We often heard secondhand of Toscanini's great admiration and affection for his orchestra, but directly from him—never!

Toscanini never hesitated to express himself freely and usually disparagingly on the subject of other conductors—there were indeed few for whom he had any real respect. "Who do they think they are, those musical assassins, changing, distorting? They think they are greater than God!" In talking about other conductors, invariably his highest seal of approval was, "He is an honest man," meaning he did not distort or cheat. He was sincere; he sought to make music, not to glorify himself. He was making music—he was being honest.

I am, of course, using the word "honest" in the particular way Toscanini used it. It was part of his Spartan "honesty" that would not permit him to sit down during a rehearsal, would not permit him to expect the men to sweat if he was not already sweating himself, would not seek an "effect" by inaccuracy or distortion. Nothing infuriates or destroys a player's sincere enthusiasm more than a conductor's demands of "Expressive!" or "Play with enthusiasm!" or "Play louder!" or "Softer!" while at the same time his whole manner belies his demands.

Sometimes conductors with the greatest sincerity and ability still have the vitality of a dead snail as they didactically tell you, "Play beautifully because it's such beautiful music!" Other conductors, though boring and matter of fact at rehearsals, become "heroic," "inspired," at performances. Some become "athletic"; they rumble with passion and tear the air to shreds with poignant and soulful gyrations. Most players look upon them with a jaundiced eye.

Any conductor can whip an orchestra to superhuman effort through terror or threat. With Toscanini, however, along with the threat and terror there was always the inspiration and self-effacement that tempered the rancor and pain he often caused others and somehow made you all the more zealously dedicated to what you were doing and more warmly affectionate toward him. That is why the men would take more from Toscanini than from any other conductor and ended up "loving" him in the process.

Some conductors take pride in "keeping cool" while they make the orchestra "play hot." Strauss, in a treatise on conducting, wrote that the "great conductors never sweat, but make the orchestra sweat." I am afraid Toscanini must indeed have been the exception that proved the rule. He sweated! "Look at me!" he often bawled out to the orchestra in a turbulent passage or during a strenuous workout. "Look at me! I'm wet!"—pointing to his sweat-drenched face, to his soaked black alpaca jacket. "I work! I sweat! And you? Shame on you! Where's your sweat? Why you not wet like me? When *I* was in the orchestra I was always hot, wet! I *tried*, not like *you*! Put something! Look at me!"

His disdain for other conductors may make him seem irrationally conceited. But to play with Toscanini was to understand what he meant. What seemed conceit was indeed truth. You had to play with most other conductors to realize what "being a good conductor," as Toscanini meant it, really consisted of. Though Toscanini was humble and self-effacing personally, he was very intolerant of what he considered the "laissez-faire" attitude of most conductors in fulfilling a composer's intentions.

Many conductors have conducted from memory, but few, if any, knew the score as Toscanini did. To him, knowing the score consisted of being conscious of every printed note, not only for itself but in its relation to the others in the phrase, and realizing how every phrase related to the work as a whole.

Following a score involves an acute knowledge of both vertical and horizontal musical relationships. It was in the vertical awareness of each thread and fiber of the whole that Toscanini stood supreme and alone. His tremendous talent in this area never ceased to be a source of complete wonder to us at rehearsals. Every note, every dynamic marking, every harmonic structure was indelibly etched in his mind. I was always conscious of the conflict that went on inside him—the frustration he felt because of the disparities between the notes on the printed score, the music in his mind's ear, and the sounds that actually came from the orchestra.

He had to make certain everything on the printed page was clearly heard in its proper place. Unerringly, Toscanini could put his finger on just that place where a passage was muddied.

"You know," he would sometimes say, stopping suddenly, "you play—I hear something—but is nothing—is a big *pasticcio* (a big mess)—I understand nothing. Come, we study." Each line would be gone over separately, each player made to play his part with utmost clarity and precision. When all was put together, so delicate, well timed, and sensitive was the balance that, instead of hearing only one or two important voices clearly, surrounded by a fog of other sounds, we heard all the voices distinctly. The music stood out in bolder relief; every note spoke; every color was brightened. It was this great gift of Toscanini's that made rehearsals so wonderfully interesting and provocative. No matter how many times we played a number, no matter how well we had rehearsed it before, Toscanini always discovered some indistinctness that needed clarifying. He never let up this intense, concentrated effort toward making "everything so clear I can touch it!" Surprisingly enough, Toscanini began this "mopping up" of a score at the point where most conductors leave off. That is why I so often felt as though I had never really heard a piece in its fullest glory until we had played it with him; for when he conducted, we heard many things clearly for the first time.

With Strauss, Wagner, and such composers of the impressionistic school as Debussy and Ravel, Toscanini would first rehearse the woodwind and brass sections separately, then the strings, all the while singing the missing melodic lines himself. Passages or runs that before were just a blur of notes became crystal clear and italicized under his prodding.

Of course, none of this was done in a matter-of-fact way. We would be playing along; suddenly he would stop short. In a foreboding voice: "*Clarinetti!* What you play!" There would be a deathly silence in the orchestra. Then, menacingly, "Play alone! *Corpo del vostro Dio!* Are you asleep? Is marked FORTE! I heard nothing! *Play alone!*" He would give the downbeat and the clarinets would play again until Toscanini fell back suddenly, as if someone had struck him. "No-o-o-o—*to-gether*—T-O-G-E-T-H-E-R! *UGUALE—not one!* Two *clarinetti*—must be EQUAL!" They would start again, then, "*No-o-o—o! Non mangiare le note! Uguale*—speak clear! Yes! You play but I understand nothing!" After some of these pointed repetitions, the obscure passages stood out in bold relief.

Sometimes the abuse aimed at a particular section would reach such heroic, explosive proportions that, like a creeping fire, it would envelop us all. We were *all* guilty! We all were careless, unknowing, unfeeling! In a gust of Italian expletives he would yell, "This is the g-r-e-a-t NBC Symphony? Hummmmmmmmph!" Then, sneeringly, "I'd like to kick each one of you in the—!"

I always marveled at the capacity of the men, particularly the first-chair players, to keep playing after such abuse. But it was the solo wind players who, because of the exposed nature of their work, drew the burden of the Old Man's tantrums. We in the string sections were usually attacked or censured as part of a group; the wind players were always alone, and their resentment often ran high. These musicians, who were outstanding artists in their fields, were gathered from the finest orchestras in the country. Other conductors praised them lavishly or corrected them with tactful suggestions, but Toscanini was completely indifferent to their eminence or to the peculiar difficulties of their instruments. To him, they were instruments in the orchestra. My admiration for their skill and control always grew as they weathered these vicious storms.

My only experience directly in the line of fire was at a rehearsal of Beethoven's *Leonore* Overture no. 3, with its celebrated unison passage for the first violins. I was sitting in the last stand then. This passage is quite a difficult one for the first violins, and Toscanini was giving it and us a thorough workout. As we played it over and over, we were becoming more and more panicky. "*Vergogna!* The worst! A disgrace! You are not *primi violini*! Not second *violini*! The *last* violins—tutti—VERGOGNA—*alone* you will play for me!" Suddenly he bellowed: "YOU! PLAY ALONE!" I looked up to see his baleful face, eyes seemingly focused in my direction. I hesitated, uncertain from the distance at whom he was actually looking. "*You*—Y-O-U!" he bellowed. "The last stand!" That removed all doubt! I lifted my violin and bow, to the audible sigh of relief of those around me who had been thinking for a horrible moment he might have meant them. The silence that descended on the orchestra was as tense as at an execution; everyone held their breath, waiting for the death trap to be sprung. He began to conduct. How I managed to get through that passage will always remain a mystery, for my fingers seemed like wet sponges and my bow suddenly weighed a ton. I had gotten halfway through when he stopped, glared at me for a moment, snorted an enigmatic—or was it disdainful?—"Hummmmph!" and bellowed *"Tutti!"* From that time on, I felt much more sympathetically toward any of those in the orchestra who found themselves unfortunately impaled on the spit of Toscanini's special personal attention.

In all the years I played with the Maestro, I cannot recall a rehearsal that was not of absorbing interest throughout. He never talked down, never expressed obvious, trite musical clichés, never wandered from the immediate point and problem, never told stories. Superior playing was taken for granted, expected, and accepted without comment. He was there to work, and no time was wasted.

One of Toscanini's most enigmatic qualities was the almost unbelievable combination of saint and demon, poet and peasant, that was such an essential and paradoxical part of his temperament. As he stood on the podium at rehearsals in his severe black alpaca jacket with a thin white piping made by a handkerchief tucked in underneath the high collar, sharply creased striped trousers, and finely shaped ankle-high slippers, he looked the personification of a priestly leader or a venerable saint. His face was transfigured with a spiritual light as he worked on a passage of surpassing beauty. He seemed lost in the mood. And suddenly, like a thunderbolt out of the blue, the saint would flee and the demon lash out at the orchestra in language that would blanch the face of a longshoreman.

I sometimes had to have some of these phrases translated before I could understand their full earthy tang and barnyard flavor. If a minister, in the midst of a sermon on the serenity of heaven, would suddenly interrupt himself to curse out roundly a parishioner who came in late, the effect could not be more startling. Toscanini had one favorite curse in Italian of purest gutter flavor that he indulged in with not too much provocation. He would hurl it with particular relish at a fellow Italian, saying, "Good! You are Italian. I don't have to explain. You know what I'm talking about!"

Once, in the middle of an outburst, he started to use this epithet, caught himself suddenly, and put his hand over his mouth. Several women were in the hall for the rehearsal. He made a grimace, glared at the player, and shouted, "Hummmmph! You know what I want to call you, but . . ." The rehearsal went on, and then the mistake was repeated. Toscanini bellowed, "*Zucconi!* (Blockheads!) I tried to be good! I tried to control myself, but you won't let me. I can't help it . . . You are a—!" Out came the epithet in full glory. He glared triumphantly at the player. A moment later, he was his angelic self again.

It was not only *what* Toscanini bellowed that gave it its special flavor but the way he said it. It was among the most horrifying sounds I have ever heard and seemed to come from his entrails. He would first almost double up, his mouth open wide, his face red, as if on the verge of an apoplectic fit. Then a raucous blast of unbelievable volume would blare forth. The only sound that comes to mind to equal it is the horrible shrieking of stuck bulls in a slaughterhouse I once visited as a boy in Chicago.

He would suddenly seize on one word—like "No!" or "Short!" or "Longer!"—and keep repeating it, slowly drawing out the vowel sound with a rising, wailing inflection until it filled the hall and all but shook the walls. We would sit there frozen, not daring to look up, staring at the floor or at the music, waiting for the storm to abate. Sometimes, in a rage, while denouncing the whole orchestra, the tirade would suddenly be directed, for no logical reason, at a particular section or individual. The innocent victim had no

recourse but to sit there and endure it. We were constantly warned the first few years never to answer back, never to try to defend ourselves or challenge him, but to let things ride.

What caused these tantrums? Sometimes it was the simplest little "error": a note too loud, a crescendo too soon—anything was enough to set off the fuse. These big scenes sometimes stemmed basically from the way he felt physically and mentally. If he were tired or disturbed about something in his private life, the ground would invariably be prepared. At other times, errors or mistakes would be accepted with unbelievable patience. Passages would be heatedly worked over, of course, but with composure, and sometimes even with wry humor. When he felt upset to begin with, anything could bring down the furies. When he was in a "good mood" and had been unusually sweet and placid (for him) for a number of weeks, we worried. "How come the Old Man's so good?" we'd wonder. "Is the sting actually going out of his bite?" Then, when a storm did blow up, we were actually relieved. "Yes, all is well. He's himself again."

Toscanini's greatest flare-ups, of which there were possibly half a dozen memorable ones, occurred when he was seized with the suspicion that the orchestra was coasting and was accepting both the music and him too casually. The first of these with the NBC Symphony occurred during our first rehearsal of the Beethoven Ninth. When we did a work of particular consequence and stature, Toscanini would come out at rehearsals a little more bristling, a little more austere and intense—even the points of his mustache appeared to stand up a little more!

The rehearsal was going along its usual dramatic way until we reached the scherzo. We were all very intent. Toscanini was driving on, covered with perspiration, when suddenly he stopped everything. "The celli!" he screamed. "The celli! Not dah-de-dah-h-h, but duy-de-dah!" Were they stupid? So-o-o-o, they were taking it easy. They were sitting back in their chairs. There was no bite, no life in their sound! They had no respect for the great music! They were asleep! They were insulting Beethoven! They were insulting *him!* No! Not with Toscanini would they play that horrible way! . . . The raging tempest was unleashed. With a torrent of insults, he broke his baton, picked up the score, began to pound it, tore it up, kicked at the stand, and then pushed it off the stage. Then, bellowing at the top of his lungs, he began to claw at his collar until his hand caught in the chain of the watch he carried in his breast pocket. With a furious wrench, he pulled it away, glared at it with unseeing eyes, and, in a vicious lunge, smashed it to the ground, where the watch spattered in all directions. N-O-O! N-O-O! He was through! Finished! He would never conduct this orchestra of jackasses again! He stomped off and walked around the outer rim of the stage, shouting his disgust and smashing his clenched fist violently down on the seats as he passed. We still heard him when he left the hall, his oaths reverberating down the corridor as he headed toward his dressing room.

For a few seconds we were petrified, hardly daring to breathe. Gradually, we looked uneasily, unbelievingly around. Nothing like this had ever happened before. What were we to do? There was still an hour of rehearsal time left. The men began muttering. What happened? What's he so excited about? "What did we do?" asked a cellist plaintively. "He could have just told us to play louder." The manager came in after a while and rather dazedly told us we were through for the day. The whole incident seemed unreal. I had heard of these rages but had always thought the reports exaggerated. I was wrong.

The next day, we assembled for rehearsal with great trepidation, expecting Toscanini to appear in the state in which he had left. In he came, smiling, looking fresh, and carrying something. As he made his way slowly along the stage, he passed our stand, stopped for a moment, and almost shyly showed us the back of a cheap Ingersoll watch he held in his hand. It was inscribed "For Rehearsals Only." He stepped to the podium, and the rehearsal was on. He was in a wonderful mood; no one would have dreamed that anything untoward had ever happened. But there was a great difference, for the orchestra never seemed so tremendously alert. Everyone was perched on the front of his chair. Yesterday's storm was in the forefront of our memories. How we gave! What a dimension that extra "beyond the call of duty" quality gave to the orchestra! Toscanini's rage somehow always achieved a musical purpose. Childish, petulant, unreasoning as it was, we somehow respected and admired his capacity to be so moved and aroused by his feeling for his work. It was as though Toscanini, through his temper, through the fear, sympathy, and resentment he inspired in the players, had made us all feel how important the music was to him and to us. There was a difference in atmosphere, and this magical atmosphere did not need any special incantation other than for Toscanini to bellow: "You! *You! Vergogna!*"

If any other conductor had even begun to speak to an orchestra the way Toscanini did, he would have been put in his place immediately. I have seen it happen. In several instances, the conductor was brought up on "charges of misbehavior" before the musicians' union, severely censured, and threatened with drastic reprisal for being too insulting or vindictive at rehearsals. But with Toscanini it was somehow different. As I have said, the men were repeatedly warned not to answer back, no matter what the provocation. "You know the Old Man," they were told. "He gets a little excited. Leave him alone, and he'll cool off. He doesn't mean it personally." When the Old Man got started, he was like a whirling dervish; it was impossible to get a rational grasp on him. Even mild apologetic protests were either completely misunderstood or served to whip him on. However, his tantrums did not have the premeditated, sadistic, sarcastic quality of lesser men. To him, the enormity of the crime of any infraction of good taste was an insult to the Muse herself—not to him personally.

Toscanini, as a conductor, through giving, driving, had to feel the counterforce and response of the orchestra's extreme effort. He could not make music any other way, and that is another reason why, in playing with him, you felt such a sense of completion and artistic fulfillment. You brought into use parts of your mind, of your skill, of your imagination, and of your body you had never thought existed. You felt the same conviction as did the Old Man. "This is great music. I must give it my greatest effort. I cannot hold back." There were few musicians indeed who did not give this special something—this innermost part of themselves—but only to the Old Man.

As a time beater, Toscanini had many superiors. As a music maker, he stood like a colossus astride the musical horizon. Though he had a fantastic "ear" and memory,

these distinctive qualities are by no means rare. It was in his capacity to make music making a monumental and epic experience, to completely exalt, to inspire every orchestra he conducted to outdo itself, to give each player the feeling that all of this was his own doing, that Toscanini's genius shone most brilliantly. The depth and fire of his intensity and his utter devotion to music melted away the callousness and the indifference that often dry the springs of music making in most hardened professional musicians. Playing with him was like a musical and spiritual regeneration. Playing beautifully—making music—became the noblest of professions and aspirations. This was the miracle of Toscanini.

Introduction

TOURING WITH TOSCANINI

IN THE LATE AFTERNOON of June 1, 1940, a thick fog enveloped the SS *Brazil* as it pulled out of New York Harbor. The VIP group of one hundred and fifty people—Arturo Toscanini, his wife, Carla, the entire NBC Symphony, RCA executives, orchestra assistants, and some wives of the musicians—were setting sail on a seven-week goodwill concert tour through South America. First stop: Rio de Janeiro!

World War II had begun in Europe the year before, and this series of concerts, sponsored by the State Department as part of the United States' Good Neighbor policy with Latin America, was an ambitious effort to show support for our South American neighbors while Europe battled Hitler. Perhaps it was a propaganda tool, perhaps a genuine cultural exchange, certainly a chance for RCA to sell more records to a new audience. Regardless of the purpose of the trip, it was clear that the passengers were anticipating an adventure as they waved goodbye to friends and family on shore.

This voyage was particularly special for my parents, Alice and Sam, who had recently married. It was to be their delayed honeymoon. They had met at a party in 1937, the year Sam joined the newly created NBC Symphony, and they quickly discovered a shared passion for the arts—as well as for one another. Since his move to New York from Chicago, Sam had devoted all his time to his career and had had little opportunity for serious romance. Alice Solomon, a Brooklyn-born artist, was recovering from a recent breakup. They had each waited a long time for the right partner to come along and had finally found their perfect match.

When I look at the picture of my parents on the ship's deck, she in her flowery hat, he in his crisp linen suit, with the Statue of Liberty slightly out of focus in the background, I see newlyweds who, at thirty and thirty-two, are radiating youth, love, and the promise of all things possible.

To my knowledge, my father never wrote about that South American summer. I couldn't find any notes beyond scribbled descriptions on the backs of the many photos he had taken during what they called their "trip of a lifetime." My mother, however, was another story.

When I dug deeper into the "Toscanini" boxes, pulling out long-forgotten treasures, I discovered a small leather-bound book with yellowing pages labeled "NBC/South America Tour/1940." I opened it and read, "First day . . . June 1" in my mother's handwriting. I had found her journal, with her daily notations from the moment they left port until their return to New York many weeks and thousands of miles later.

It didn't take me long to decipher my mother's faded pencil entries and recognize her familiar conversational writing style. As I read through the journal, I felt as if she were sitting next to me, telling me the stories about their exotic travels to Rio, Buenos Aires, Montevideo, and São Paulo. I was also struck by the realization that she had carefully preserved this diary for so many decades, never dreaming that her casual jottings would one day be read with such scrutiny.

On the trip, my mother was one of ten "orchestra wives"—her quaint expression to describe spouses of the men in the orchestra. Did she feel self-conscious or out of place? As far as I can tell, not for a second. She easily bonded with the other women, and, I'm convinced, thanks to her quick wit and style, she was also welcomed by the more than one hundred men in the group.

Their first days on board were filled with "awe-inspiring" scenery and fun-in-the-sun shipboard activities, as well as the constant *click click click* of cameras whenever Toscanini stopped to mingle with the group during one of his daily strolls on deck.

In the evenings, my parents dressed up in their "swanky best" for a night of dancing, card games, rumba lessons, or screenings of the latest movies. I can see why Mom and Dad turned heads whenever they entered a room—he with his easy, accessible charm and handsome demeanor, she beaming with pride and love when her arm was linked in his.

In the photograph of them on deck, they look, to me, like a golden couple. Ever since I can remember, their names were always uttered as one word: Sam-and-Alice, Alice-and-Sam.

But for all the buzz about the journey ahead, my mother wrote, "There is an ever present overtone of fear." The United States had not yet entered the war, but the passengers could never forget that "we were on the open sea, in wartime, and anything could happen." One of the many circulating rumors that made everyone anxious was, "The boat is silently controlled by a few Nazis on the crew, who dominate the captain!"

"A.T. walks around fingering a crucifix praying for the Allies." On June 10, when it was announced that Italy had declared war on Great Britain and had attacked France, "A.T. ran out of the dining room up to his cabin . . . and stayed there for two days. He is so depressed over the world news." As an émigré from Mussolini's persecution in Italy, Toscanini doubted he would ever see his homeland again. (He did finally return to Milan in 1946 to conduct at La Scala.)

Rehearsals were cancelled. Instead, there were lectures by the captain on how to be on your guard in South America. "Don't speak to anyone or criticize anything. Be suspicious. Always." A few shaky weeks lay ahead.

Even though an ominous cloud of concern hung over them, the group was received with enormous fanfare and treated as royalty upon arrival in each city. There were endless rounds of cocktail parties, embassy receptions, private tours, and invitations to the homes of the rich and famous. Every concert was a triumph in spite of some disruptive heckling from Nazi sympathizers in the audience, who shouted, "Il Duce! Il Duce!" or "Jew orchestra!" The orchestra played to sold-out crowds; some people waited in line for days hoping for a ticket. Standing ovations often lasted as long as pieces on the program. The concerts in Montevideo were particular highlights. "Last concert tonight—and what an ovation—15 minutes!"

On the voyage home, the group, sated and exhausted, was buoyed up by the stunning success of their tour and by Toscanini's jubilant gratitude. However, after so many weeks traveling under a wartime threat, they were relieved to see the familiar silhouette of Lady Liberty as they approached New York Harbor.

Right: St. Louis, Missouri.
Opposite: Denver, Colorado.

Ten years later, in 1950, soon after my dad's *Saturday Review* article "Playing with the Maestro" was published, the NBC Symphony went on another major tour. This time it was a ten-thousand-mile road trip on a private train, the orchestra performing twenty-one concerts in twenty cities across the United States. The fervent audiences numbered almost a hundred thousand, all big fans of the orchestra from their many seasons of listening to radio broadcasts and recordings and, more recently, of viewing the concerts on television. They gave Toscanini an exuberant welcome when the "Toscanini Special" pulled into their town. As my father said in a newspaper interview during the tour, "They greeted Toscanini as a friend, rather than a big shot star."

"Think of it," he said in another interview. "Toscanini is eighty-three. But he never looks back, only to the future. And this was his attitude on the tour. He always wanted to know what the next town was, what kind of stage it had, what was interesting about the countryside we were passing through."

My mother did not get to go on this tour. She had her hands full with five-year-old me, but Dad's letters home arrived almost daily. He wrote on the train, in the hotels, before a rehearsal, after a concert—whenever he could jot down some news:

> *. . . In San Francisco the audience leaped to their feet, shouting "Bravo!"*
> *as Toscanini walked on stage. He was particularly moved.*

. . . We have played two concerts in a row—last night in Portland—tonight in Seattle, then two nights on the train. Travel—rehearsal—sightsee—concert—ovation—travel . . .

. . . I'm writing this after the concert in Richmond. As an encore we played "Dixie." Twice! Did you hear the yell all the way up to New York?!

They went on to play "Dixie" two more times—in Atlanta and New Orleans. Always a foot-stomping showstopper. But it wasn't until after the third concert that the true meaning of the song was brought to Toscanini's attention. Once he learned of its association with slavery in the Old South, he refused to play it ever again.

For years after, my father would say that the 1950 cross-country tour was "easily the most inspiring experience" he had ever had.

Chapter Two

TOURING WITH TOSCANINI

IN 1950 WE GAVE twenty-one magnificent concerts in every part of the United States—no vacation trip could have been more enjoyable. We saw great snow-capped mountains, vast deserts, and exciting cities. We ate at Antoine's and had doughnuts at the Morning Call in New Orleans, stayed at the Shamrock in Houston, saw San Francisco from the Top of the Mark, ogled the stars in Hollywood, watched huge Columbia River salmon shoot the rapids at Bonneville Dam, and spent an unforgettable day at Sun Valley. In Cleveland we even saw Joe DiMaggio hit a home run with bases loaded.

As the tour progressed, as the beauty and wonder of our great country unfolded, we realized that the greatest wonder of all was riding on the train with us—our incredible eighty-three-year-old Maestro, Toscanini himself. Throughout the trip, his zest and enthusiasm, his physical and emotional endurance, astounded us all, even those of us who had known and played with him for years. At times the Old Man seemed so tired and gray with fatigue after a concert that we wondered how in the world he would keep going. But the next day he would appear as upbeat and chipper as ever, looking so fresh we could hardly believe our eyes.

Wherever there was something unusual to see, a famous restaurant to visit, something of interest to experience, Toscanini would be there, enjoying himself immensely. His curiosity seemed insatiable. I had never seen him so happy, so carefree and fun-loving as he was on this trip, so deeply touched and demonstrative in his appreciation of the attention and ovations that greeted him everywhere.

After the taxing journey, with six weeks of touring and twenty-one strenuous concerts under his belt, one would think that our Maestro might take a rest. Not Toscanini! Two days after we returned, he gave a party for all the musicians and their wives at his home in Riverdale, New York. He warmly and enthusiastically greeted each of the some three hundred of us present and did not sit down in the four hours we were there. "You know," he told me, "I don't feel a bit tired; maybe I should have conducted more concerts!" The next two nights we put in hours of recording, and a day later he left for concert engagements in Europe. Is it any wonder, then, that our Old Man and his incredible stamina were the dominant topics of discussion among the players? "How does he do it . . . !"

Our private train, and the care that was taken of all of us, made this trip truly deluxe, unequaled in comfort and luxury within the memory of the many of us who had traveled before. The fourteen cars were made up of compartments and roomettes, lounge cars and diners, with Toscanini's private car—either by chance or design called "Columbus"—bringing up the rear. Another Italian was discovering America! Various services were at our disposal at all times, with even prearranged laundry pickups along the way. In the cities where transportation was at all in doubt, buses took us to and from the concert halls. After each concert, a light buffet supper was provided on the train. Toward the end of the trip, between Washington and Philadelphia, there was an all-night party for the orchestra en route. This party was also the occasion for the presentation of gifts from the orchestra to two RCA officials who managed the tour, in appreciation of the wonderful time and the consideration that had been shown us. Special birthday parties for the men were given everywhere, with Toscanini often joining in.

The train once halted at about two in the morning while we were going through New Mexico, and I was amazed to find that we had stopped to pick up a birthday cake that had been ordered by wire for a party the next day. The whole trip moved along with such regularity and precision that once, when the train ground to a sudden stop while crossing the desert in Arizona and word spread that one of the engines had sprung an oil leak, we all piled out in great excitement, hoping some "adventure" had finally turned up. Gleeful visions of outlaws, rattlesnakes, and starvation and thirst in the desert rudely vanished as a relief engine came chugging into view in about ten minutes. This was the only mishap in an otherwise perfect train trip.

Our day of "rest" in Sun Valley was the high spot of the tour. As we arrived early in the morning, we were awakened by the gunshots of a "holdup" gang of cowboys riding around the train. The local high school band, in full uniform, was blasting away. In no time at all, to the delight of the youngsters and the consternation of the bandmaster, some of our boys had grabbed the band's instruments and parts of uniforms and were playing away madly. Soon after, we were all over the landscape—swimming, skating, and bicycling. At ten in the morning, I came upon Toscanini, stretched out full length on the lawn, drinking a toast in champagne to the beautiful mountains. Later that day, while up on the ten-thousand-foot Mount Baldy, we were amazed to see him coming up the ski tow, and we broke into a cheer as his chair swung into view. The jaunty beret on his head and his waving arms gave him the appearance of a happy boy playing hooky. He brushed aside any concern about him and turned anxiously toward the rest of his party who were just coming into sight. "The others—I hope they're all right?"

"Maestro," I said to him, "you are a brave man. Some of the boys were afraid to come up."

He looked at me very earnestly and said, "I've never been afraid of anything in my life. I like to try everything." All through the day, he was "one of the boys," joining us in a marvelous outdoor barbecue and applauding the buffoonery of the "Sad Symphony" performed with pots, pans, and kazoos by the men, who were burlesquing the numbers we had been playing on the tour. We cheered wildly as he rather dazedly accepted an invitation to lead us in "The Stars and Stripes Forever." That night, a more exhausted, happier, lobster-red group of musicians could not have been found.

Ours was no tour bringing culture to the "musically starved backwoods" of America. On the contrary, I felt that our appearances were in the nature of a testimonial to the great musical development and achievements that have taken place in every part of our country. Every city we visited but one had a flourishing symphony orchestra and a proud musical tradition of its own. Wherever we played, we found sophisticated, musically aware audiences such as I had snobbishly thought existed only in New York. We had prepared six different programs to be performed during the trip. Interestingly enough, many of those scheduled had to be changed as the tour progressed, since various cities began to send in requests for the more "serious" programs.

In spite of our holiday spirit while we were actually traveling, there was no such feeling when it came to the concerts themselves. Every performance was played with all the dedication that so marked Toscanini. And with Toscanini himself so relaxed, we all let go con amore; everyone played with his whole heart. The performances all along were undoubtedly the finest I ever heard our orchestra give. No wonder Toscanini was delighted and pleased as I had never seen him before. It was always intriguing to hear how differently the orchestra sounded in each auditorium. The halls we enjoyed playing in most from an acoustical standpoint were the Lyric in Baltimore, the Opera House in San Francisco, and the Academy of Music in Philadelphia. We were all particularly on edge for these performances, and I believe they represented the musical high points of the tour. It was also very interesting to feel the ebb and flow, the little subtle changes that took place every time we played a program over again. The programs were always fresh, never static in their repetition. All were wonderful. All were different.

As the tour went on, Toscanini seemed to become more and more informal. For the first time, he began to appear at rehearsals without the little high-collared black jacket; instead, he wore a regular white shirt, minus collar and tie.

Rehearsals were brief. Their sole purpose was to get the "feel" and "sound" of the halls we were in. Toscanini would italicize a note here, a phrase there, saying, so characteristically, "You know—is nothing . . . but is something!" He would cut the rehearsal short, saying, "You know it. I know it. See you tonight."

He never went out into the hall to hear the orchestra, always saying that if it sounded good to him up on the stand, it would sound all right back in the auditorium. Once, at a rehearsal in Richmond, the Old Man called out to those at the rear of the hall, "Is good?"

"Sounds wonderful, Maestro," came back.

"Humph," said the Old Man, "is funny . . . sounds like a *pasticcio* here and they tell me wonderful!"

The orchestra was shifted around, a few platforms were adjusted, and we played again. "Can you hear the woodwinds?" called out the Old Man.

"Wonderful, Maestro."

"Can you hear the clarinet?"

". . . Well, the clarinet could be stronger."

"Just tell me if you hear it," yelled the Old Man impatiently. "I'll decide if it should be louder or softer!"

Strangely, the largest halls were in the smaller cities, where audiences ranged from four to twelve thousand. Many were of the oddest shape and size: the gymnasium of the University of Texas in Austin; the huge auditorium in Atlanta; the gaudy Fox movie theater in St. Louis; the unusual auditorium in Denver made up of two halls put together, with the stage for the orchestra improvised in the center, surrounded by the audience; and the mammoth hall in Cleveland, where we played to our largest audience, twelve thousand persons.

At a rehearsal the day before our concert in Austin, while working on a Rossini overture, Toscanini complained about the percussion player's part. *"Dio santo!"* he exclaimed. "Is not right!" In time for the performance the next day, he had written out, by hand and from memory, the correct percussion part.

In Atlanta, an incident occurred that illustrates Toscanini's almost mystical attitude toward music. As we entered the huge auditorium in the morning for rehearsal, we were greeted by the smell of horses and manure. (There had been a horse show a few days before.) In the center of the auditorium was a large prizefight ring, erected for the fights that were to take place that night; our own concert was to be played the next night. Workmen were milling about on the stage, building extensions, setting the scene, as it were. We all assembled on the stage for rehearsal. All the noise, hammering, and bustle stopped, of course, when Toscanini came to the stand. After a brief rehearsal, Toscanini stepped off the stand and approached Walter, his son, as the workmen reappeared and began working on the stage. At that moment, a foreman of the stagehands walked past, with his hat on his head, and began to set up the railing around the podium. Toscanini stopped abruptly. His face hardened. With a flick of his stick he knocked off the workman's hat. "*Ignorante!*—Take off the hat! Is a church here!" The man, struck dumb with amazement, looked about, stared at the prizefight ring, sniffed the manure-saturated air, and looked at the Old Man with perplexed terror. "Yes! *Ignorante!*" rasped the Old Man. "Where is music is a church! Off with the hat, *stupido!*"

When Toscanini got off the train for brief stops, he always wore his beret, though dressed impeccably in his suede-and-leather shoes, starched collar, and a florid tie. He enjoyed tremendously mingling and talking to everyone about anything, although the conversation invariably turned to music. An enthusiastic, gesticulating figure, he would always be found with a group of us gathered around. Even backstage, before a concert, moving about restlessly before going on, he would engage some of the men in conversation.

Throughout the trip, chefs of the hotels we stayed at made a point of seeking him out. Many of them were Italian, and the Old Man was always particularly delighted to speak to them. The chef of the Book-Cadillac in Detroit gave Toscanini a beautiful portrait of himself in chocolate and icing, on which he had worked for three weeks. This striking likeness of his head occupied a place of honor on a table in his home at the party he gave when he returned from the tour.

The devotion and care of Walter Toscanini for his father were very touching. He always hovered around him in his role of secretary, personal representative, and companion. He would kiss the Old Man on the cheek just before Toscanini walked out on the stage. Strangely enough, when it came to taking pictures, there was no greater "camera bug" than Walter himself, his pet subject being no different from ours—the Maestro. Whenever a stop was made at some particular point of interest, Toscanini would appear and immediately be surrounded by the men, cameras clicking away like castanets. He did not mind at all. Even when we paused for about a half hour at beautiful Mount Shasta in northern California, more pictures were taken of Toscanini than of the mountain.

Toscanini and his son Walter.

Surrounded by the barrage of camera fans, the usually camera-shy Toscanini suddenly called out, "Where's Cooley?" (Carleton Cooley, our first viola player and number-one camera fan.) "He wanted to take pictures of me . . . and now where is he?" After we returned to New York, I once asked Toscanini if he had seen any of the pictures of the tour. He said, "No . . . you know, I hate to read about myself or even see the pictures of myself . . . even when I shave or put on my tie I hate to look in the mirror!"

Scenes backstage before and after a concert were often laughable and bizarre, not to say embarrassing, with cameramen from the local papers prowling around for candid-camera shots. With few of the halls equipped to handle one hundred men changing into dress clothes, most of us changed right on the stage behind the backdrop. In Portland, all that separated our "dressing room" from the public was a thin, almost gauzelike drape. To our horror, we found that with each passing breeze, the supposedly protective curtain would be partly exposing us to the interested eyes of the audience. In Richmond, one of the men almost collapsed when he found he had been dressing in full view of a young lady in the box on the other side of the stage. While in Denver, groups of people were outside the auditorium; I thought they were waiting for standing room. They were merely watching the musicians parade about in their underwear! While rather skittish at first, we later became quite hardened and reconciled to finding our dressing rooms public domain.

A more gratifying and exciting finale to the tour could not be imagined than the last concert in Philadelphia. With the final encore, "The Stars and Stripes Forever," almost drowned out by the incessant cheering, a man in the second row began screaming in Italian, "Toscanini! . . . *Speranza del mondo!* . . . *Luce d'Italia!*" and waving the huge audience to its feet. The ovation was one of the most fervent and brilliant of the tour. I later saw this man backstage, trying to get in to see Toscanini, and I called out to him, "*Bravo!* You were a wonderful audience!" He looked at me in surprise and said, "Don't thank me. It's from the heart!" "From the heart" seemed to be the feeling of all the audiences that greeted us from coast to coast.

As a souvenir of the trip, Toscanini gave us a happy, smiling picture of himself taken on the ski tow in Sun Valley. He inscribed: "Sweet remembrance of our unforgettable tour."

RECORDING WITH TOSCANINI

LIFE IN MY FAMILY revolved around the challenging schedule of my father's rehearsals, performances, and, most especially, arduous RCA recording sessions. Dad would come home ragged but enthusiastic from those long days with a whole new string of Italian curses added to his repertoire. *Vergogna!*, one of Toscanini's favorite expressions, became a household word for us. I loved to repeat it with great theatrics as often as I could.

Dad spent hours practicing his violin. I loved to listen to him rehearse the same few bars over and over, perfecting his bowing technique for a Mozart symphony or conquering a complicated fingering sequence for a Wagner overture. I would hover just outside the double doors of our living room, hoping to catch a glimpse of him—his violin perched under his chin, bow in hand. I can still picture the stern look on my mother's face as she held a finger to her lips, making us talk in whispers and walk on tiptoe around the house.

He had been playing the violin since he was six. He couldn't remember when he didn't have a fiddle in his hands. Where had this musical gift come from? His parents, Jewish immigrants who had fled Ukraine to settle in Chicago, were not particularly musical. I've found no clue about who introduced little "Sammy" to his first violin or who, once he started to play, first recognized his extraordinary talent. When his parents were told he was a musical prodigy, they barely grasped what that meant. Fortunately, they listened and found the money to engage the best private teachers in the city. From that point on, much of Sam's young life was devoted to making music.

GRISHA BORUSHEK

Eminent Russian Violin Pedagogue

PRESENTS

SAMUEL ANTEK

ARTIST PUPIL

—IN—

VIOLIN RECITAL

Sunday Afternoon, March 8th, 2:30 p. m.

—AT—

KIMBALL CONCERT HALL

Wabash Ave. at Jackson Boulevard

Tickets 50c and $1.10

Procured at Kimball Hall Box Office and
Northwestern Conservatory of Music, 2753 West North Avenue

He made his first appearance as a soloist at the age of sixteen in Chicago—the family celebrity! Determined to make music his future, he moved to New York before he was twenty and landed a prized opportunity to be a protégé of the famed violinist and teacher Leopold Auer. That pivotal experience led to a grant for further study at the Juilliard Foundation, now known as the Juilliard School. After such a stellar education with great masters, he began to concertize, as well as to enjoy some high-profile showcase moments—which not only helped to pay expenses but earned him some valuable press attention.

Soon after, in 1936, he had his long-awaited debut at Manhattan's Town Hall, followed by a year of solo recitals. I can only imagine how proud he must have felt to receive such laudatory praise for his work: "rare purity and beauty," "magnificent skill," "the soul of an artist." He was now an acknowledged virtuoso!

Within a year, Sam, still in his twenties, received the pivotal invitation that would change the course of his life. In 1937, he was asked to join an elite group of musicians who were being assembled for RCA's ambitious new enterprise, the NBC Symphony. As Harvey Sachs states in his Toscanini biography, Toscanini wrote to a friend after the first NBC concert: "The strings are first class, beyond any description!"

The NBC Symphony started recording a year later in 1938. As my father recounts in the following chapter, the orchestra struggled through what we now would consider archaic methods to achieve the quality of their vibrant live radio broadcasts.

Today, we live in a digital world with sophisticated studio equipment and home recording software just a few clicks away. With another tap, we can download any artist, from Jascha Heifetz to Jay Z. We don't think about what it was like to make a recording in the late 1930s and early 1940s—before long-playing records, before magnetic tape, and before stereo sound. Even as recording methods made enormous advances during the following decades, the painstaking process of recording with the NBC Symphony, first in studio 8H and later in Carnegie Hall, was exhausting for both Toscanini and the musicians. Sometimes it meant hours performing take after take, repeating and rerecording a section of a piece many times until the Maestro, the players, and the RCA engineers were satisfied. Toscanini knew that once a recording was completed, it would be a reflection of their artistic efforts forever—a concept with which he was never completely comfortable.

It is our great good fortune that, through the efforts of the Toscanini family and dedicated music lovers, many of these recordings, as well as transcriptions of the live radio and television broadcasts, have successfully survived. They have been preserved, remastered, repackaged, and digitized. The CDs and videos are still in demand online, offering new audiences the richness and immediacy from that historic era.

Preparing for a recording session.

Chapter 3

RECORDING WITH TOSCANINI

THROUGHOUT THE YEARS OF my association with Toscanini and the NBC Symphony, I participated in all but one of their recording sessions. Our first with Toscanini was in 1938, when we did the Haydn Symphony no. 88 in Studio 8H, and our last numbing session took place at Carnegie Hall shortly after the final concert in 1954. On the whole, recording sessions were less tense than concerts; they had the more relaxed atmosphere of rehearsals. Engineers from RCA Victor, of course, had worked for hours before the appointed time, preparing the auditorium with strategically placed microphones; for acoustical purposes, materials were draped over large blocks of seats and the boxes. Just in front of Toscanini was the red "go" signal—a small bulb on top of a rod about four feet high, placed directly in the Old Man's line of vision.

The usual routine before the actual recording session was somewhat like this:

A few moments before Toscanini appeared on the podium, Jimmy Dolan, the librarian, would come bustling out with an open score in his hand, and the concertmaster, amid the hubbub of tuning, practicing, and conversation, would call out, "Here they are . . . Here are the 'stops.'" These "stops" were indications as to stopping points in the music, which, for purposes of record length, had been arranged at the necessary places. These would vary in length. In those days before long-playing records, the timing had to be quite exact, geared to the approximate five-minute length of a twelve-inch record side. With the advent of tape for recording and its techniques for splicing, stops became much less necessary.

The noises of the orchestra would die down as Jimmy called out the places in the music that had been earmarked for these time breaks. While he gave such directions as, "First stop is ten bars after letter D—play the downbeat of the bar and then stop. The next stop is at letter H," the men at each stand would mark these directions into their parts. Invariably, there was a bit of confusion as someone would call out, "Did you say D or E?"

"D," Jimmy would call out again.

The stops were planned very carefully by Toscanini and the recording director, always taking into consideration musical as well as technical details so that a stop would not occur within a phrase or, worse, in the midst of a musical climax. At the very beginning of a session, Toscanini sometimes would say to us, "The stop is clear, no?" "*Si*, yes!" we would answer. But there would always be somebody who asked for clarification. Sometimes the concertmaster would say, "Maestro, let's play it to be sure." Toscanini would then indicate for us to start a few bars before the proposed stop and we would play it through. I always marveled that Maestro himself never made any mistakes, that he never forgot where a stop was.

As we approached the stop, Toscanini never gave a sign to the orchestra. He would suddenly cut us off at precisely the right spot, or sometimes, in a gleeful manner, he would clap both arms across his chest as though to cut off the sound. At such times, his face would light up like that of a playful, pleased child.

There was usually a small loudspeaker at Toscanini's feet, so that the engineers in the recording room could communicate with him. However, when there was any important question to discuss—a problem of balance or timing—the recording director generally came to Toscanini at the podium and whispered his suggestions. It was part of protocol and respect for the Old Man not to shout out any instructions to him on the public address system. On his right was a high microphone that he could use if he wanted to say something to the engineer or the recording director. It was amusing to see Toscanini bend down almost to the floor toward the loudspeaker from which the recording director's voice issued and talk to it as if there were really a person in that box.

Toscanini never seemed interested in the actual mechanics of recording, and over the years his methods of recording never changed, in spite of all the advances in electronics and recording techniques. He seemed concerned solely in what he or we did musically and judged the recording only by what he heard on the playback. This was quite different from Stokowski, Reiner, Walter, or any other conductor with whom I have ever played. All of them were concerned in varying degrees with the mechanics and made suggestions to the engineer and the men of the orchestra about "playing differently in front of a microphone." This was particularly the case after they had heard the playback in the control room.

Very often, after finishing the first take, the recording director would call out over the loudspeaker, "Maestro, would you like to do another?" or "Would you like to hear this one?" The Old Man, somewhat bewildered by the blatant quality of the voice on the public address system, would turn to the orchestra rather uncertainly. "They want to know if they should play it back for you here, Maestro," some of the men near him would call out. "*Si, bene, bene,* play. . ." the Old Man would say in the general direction of the speaker at his feet. "Yes! Maestro wants to hear it," several men would chorus out triumphantly. I say "triumphantly" because when a take was played back on the stage, it not only gave the men a chance to rest and hear themselves but to listen on "company time," so to speak. Usually the playback occurred during the orchestra's allotted rest time within each hour, but whenever it was possible, for practical as well as artistic reasons, we sometimes encouraged the Old Man to ask to have the playback immediately. The longer the session lasted, the better!

As the music was fed back into the auditorium of Carnegie Hall through a loudspeaker raised up over the seats, everything would become deathly quiet. The Old Man would refuse the proffered chair and remain on the stand or step off to the floor of the stage; occasionally, he would sit on the edge of the podium, slumped over in an attitude of great weariness.

The music would begin, and the men, though in various positions of relaxation, would sit motionless, following the music with their eyes. As the sound poured forth,

players grimaced or pursed their lips dubiously when certain passages they were particularly involved in failed to sound right. Some beamed at points, looking around to receive a nod of approval from their fellow musicians. These signs on such occasions were a gesture of twirling a mustache like a dandy or the shuffling of feet as a sign of applause. Eventually, however, everybody's eyes focused on the Old Man.

As he listened, Toscanini became oblivious of everything around him but the sound. His head was uplifted, his eyes unseeing, staring toward the ceiling. This particular stance of Toscanini, aside from its extraordinary spiritual aura, gave an impression of great concentration. Sometimes, in rhythmic, dramatic music, Toscanini would frown as he listened and would even begin to conduct the playback, going through all his flowing movements and giving cues to the players; the tempo and pulse had to sound right to his muscles as well as to his ears. Toscanini never made any comment about the beauty or texture of the sound in the recording; his attention was always focused on the tempo, drive, and orchestral balance.

Actually, there were three different times for playback. The first was the one I have described above. Often, though, it would take place during the twenty-minute rest period. The second would be when Maestro listened in either his dressing room or the recording room while he himself was resting. And lastly there was the playback in his house in Riverdale, where he could listen at his leisure over the elaborate sound system that had been set up.

The actual procedure for making a recording in the studio followed this routine. After Toscanini had arrived at the podium, he would rehearse for a few moments, clarifying difficult sections of a particular piece or going over some part that had been performed well at the preceding concert. Sometimes he would start at the beginning of a piece and continue to the first stop. If all went well, he might say, "I think is good, no? We try. . ." and bend down toward the loudspeaker close to his feet. "Ready, ready!" he would croak throatily with good-natured impatience. Of course, the engineers could not hear him, for he was talking into the speaker and not into the microphone. Back would come the voice of the recording engineer: "Are you ready, Maestro?" "Ready! Ready!" the Old Man would repeat impatiently. "Maestro, can we hear just a bit of the beginning for balance?" "*Sì! Sì!*" the Old Man would reply. We would start, and after a few bars, the voice of the engineer would cut through raucously, "That's fine, sounds fine, Maestro," startling the Old Man, who by that time was already immersed in the music. Toscanini would then sometimes shrug his shoulders, making an overelaborate gesture with his arms, as if to say, "Thank you! Glad you liked it!" "We'll make one! Quiet, everybody," the engineer would call out. An eerie silence would descend as the musicians sat motionless, their instruments poised. The low, monotonous voice of the engineer would come through the loudspeaker like a priest intoning a chant: "RCA no. 121211, take one." The Old Man would stand there with his hands raised, his eyes fastened on the little bulb that gave the signal to begin. Each second seemed endless. Suddenly, the bulb would light up, the Old Man would glance around quickly, hesitate a moment, give the downbeat, and we were off!

At the first prearranged stop, Toscanini would cut off the orchestra abruptly, and we would all literally stop in our tracks, motionless, frozen, instruments still held in playing position. Toscanini, too, would hold his arms poised in midair. After a few moments of silence, the little red bulb would go out, to indicate that the actual recording was over. Suddenly there would be a babble of voices, of coughing, of clearing of throats, as the men relaxed, picking up previous conversations and discussing various aspects of the performance.

Sometimes, no sooner was the little bulb out than Toscanini would pounce upon an individual player or a group, furious over some detail. Occasionally, even during the actual recording, a violent pantomime would take place as Toscanini, upset by something that was not right, found himself completely frustrated by the fact that he could not yell and ruin the recording. He would go through frenzied gestures to indicate, "I'll remember you when this is over!" and as soon as it was possible, he would burst out with a stream of violent abuse and invective. On rare occasions, he would let himself go in spite of the fact that the light was on, yelling and cursing because of some inaccuracy or fancied stupidity, then stop abruptly when he realized what he had done. As he would stand there silently fuming for a moment, the voice of the engineer would ingratiatingly come through the loudspeaker: "Would you like to make another one, Maestro?" The Old Man would glare in exasperation, shrugging his shoulders with a resigned air, and say, "Yes . . . make . . . make!" The monotonous voice would announce the "take" once more, and the whole procedure would be repeated.

The atmosphere of recording sessions was essentially the same as that of rehearsals: Toscanini's general attitude would be the determining factor. But he often gave the impression that he resented recording in general and felt it was a sort of necessary evil. Above all, however, he seemed to feel a bitterness and self-disillusionment concerning his own accomplishment, as though the recordings were a candid mirror of his music making and he was quite unhappy about what he saw. What came "out" was, as it were, never quite like what went "in"—what he imagined he was producing. During the early years of recording, he often would insist he had not conducted a piece in *that* way, that the machine was distorting it; the engineer and the microphones were persecuting him!

In every recording session, Toscanini would start out bravely enough, but as he listened to the playbacks, he would wilt. I used to ache with sympathy for him, and as the session progressed, he would seem to become almost indifferent and withdrawn, anxious to get it over with. When the engineer would ask for another take after two had already been made, the Old Man would querulously cry, "Why, is good enough, no? You have two, no? Why again? *Per Dio santo!*" Sometimes the engineer would explain that there had been some technical difficulty "upstairs" or that there had been some noise—a cough or the scraping of a chair. Usually, though, the Old Man cooperated with remarkable patience and strength, often repeating a section three or four times.

At recording sessions, just as in both rehearsal and concert, Toscanini always gave his utmost, both physically and emotionally. Even though we would make as many as four takes, he would constantly maintain his same level of intensity. And all this when he was in his eighties! During a particularly long session, he would often say to the men, "We must play again. Something . . . I don't know . . ." A groan would come from the players—"Again?"—and some of them, particularly the brass, would point to their lips to indicate they were tired. Occasionally, one would go right up to the Old Man on the podium to say that he needed a rest, that his lips were numb. Sometimes, Toscanini would flare up at the engineer: "Why? Why? We play three times! Is enough, no? You say is good; why we need play again?" Then he might go off into a tirade in Italian at no one in particular, screaming about how he hated recording, how he was wasting his time.

No matter how tired we were, the sight of the Old Man, exhausted but giving everything he had, always served as a source of inspiration to us.

One has to play through a major work, such as a score of Wagner's, several times to understand how both Toscanini and the orchestra would feel in such instances. I remember that after rehearsing a Wagnerian piece and recording it a few times, Toscanini was asked for yet another take of this exhausting number. I sat in my seat and marveled that, though obviously annoyed, he acquiesced. I felt sure that, tired as he was, he would merely begin the number and ride along with the orchestra, for the men knew it so well they could have played it in their sleep. I hoped that, for once, he would take it easy, but such was not the case. As the piece started, he was off again, with the greatest of effort, slashing and pumping through each wave of sound.

When it was over, he stood there, arms hanging limp at his sides, too spent to move or speak. *"Basta!"* he whispered throatily, slowly, as though with painful effort. "Enough!" He dropped his baton on the stand with a gesture of finality and stepped off laboriously, his legs so stiff from standing that he almost stumbled. He wound his way heavily through the orchestra, while all the men moved silently to let him pass.

Introduction
A VISIT WITH TOSCANINI

IF THE 1920s AND 1930s were the decades for Dad's recognition as a virtuoso violinist, the 1940s and 1950s were the years in which he finally fulfilled his lifelong aspiration to conduct.

He had been conducting many small ensembles for a while, but his first important opportunity came about in an unexpected way. After his Town Hall violin debut, he was engaged as a guest soloist on the *General Foods Radio Hour*, a weekly live radio program featuring symphonic, popular, and operatic music. On the day of the broadcast, the conductor became ill and couldn't go on, and, just like a scene from a Hollywood movie in which the young hopeful is plucked from the chorus to replace the ailing star, my father was asked to take over. The broadcast was so successful that he became their regular conductor for the next few years, conducting hundreds of weekly programs. This achievement further energized his ambition to one day conduct a major symphony orchestra.

That day came in 1947, when Dad received a long-hoped-for appointment. He was named musical director and conductor of the New Jersey Symphony Orchestra. Founded in 1922, the NJSO, a state orchestra, was in need of new and energetic leadership. Samuel Antek, only thirty-eight, was the perfect choice. From then on, he held two illustrious and concurrent positions—playing the violin in the NBC Symphony and conducting his own orchestra.

FEBRUARY 10. 1949

N. J. Symphony Was Delightful

Technically Varied Concert
Forcefully Conducted
by Samuel Antek.

List, Antek Share Honors at Concert

Pianist Heard as Soloist with
N. J. Symphony.

New Jersey Symphony Orchestra

SAMUEL ANTEK, Musical Director

Two of thi
sical organiz
night in Ora
New Jersey
segment of F
host to the
established i
their joint m
raptured app
capacity aud

Symphony Appears

New Jersey Group Assisted by Upsala Choir in
Concert at Orange High School

The Montclair Times

THURSDAY, NOVEMBER 20, 1947

Capacity Audience Hails New Symphony Conductor

N. J. Symphony Orchestra Scores Triumph in Concert

SAMUEL ANTEK
Conductor of the New Jersey Symphony

The reviews for his 1947 NJSO inaugural concert were raves:

*New blood and new spirit, mainly in the person of Samuel Antek, rising young
American conductor, led a capacity audience to cheer the opening of the twenty-
sixth season of the New Jersey Symphony Orchestra. . . . In a manner reminiscent
of the greeting inspired at the start of a new era or the discovery of a new star.*

—*The Montclair Times*

*Springing phoenix-like from the ashes of its former self, The New Jersey
Symphony Orchestra presented a new face and a new conductor to a large,
eager audience last night. . . . The result, in a word, was a wow.*

—*The Newark Evening News*

For the next ten years, Sam dedicated himself to raising the profile of the orchestra, attracting world-class musicians and famed soloists while developing crowd-pleasing programs. His goal was to give the orchestra a broader presence throughout New Jersey by bringing concerts into more communities and drawing in more people, especially those who had never before attended a live musical event.

Dad's ambitious leadership of the New Jersey Symphony Orchestra was widely admired. But to my young eyes, his crowning achievement was his innovative Saturday morning concert series for children, "Music for Fun," which he launched in 1950—years before Leonard Bernstein. On those special Saturdays, we piled into the car and headed off to Maplewood or Montclair or the Oranges, or to whatever New Jersey town was hosting the concert. Sometimes, I'd sit in the audience, surrounded by a thousand other kids. More often, I preferred watching from the wings.

My father's programs gave the children, including me, the thrill of hearing music come alive. With his warm enthusiasm and informal style, Dad delighted the kids who sat on the edge of their seats in rapt attention as they were introduced to Leroy Anderson's classic "The Syncopated Clock," Prokofiev's symphonic fairy tale *Peter and the Wolf*, or John Philip Sousa's rousing "The Stars and Stripes Forever." He told them stories about the composers and the instruments, and then, particularly entertaining for them, he engaged them in interactive games with the players to learn about tempo and rhythm.

At intermission, Dad came offstage, dripping with perspiration, his adrenaline pumping. (It has been said that the exertion of conducting is the equivalent of chopping down a tree!) My mother was always ready with a towel and dry shirt. He'd spend a few minutes catching his breath and cooling off. Then back he'd go to his eager young fans, who quieted down the minute he strode onstage for the second half.

At the end of the concert, I'd stand backstage beaming with that's-my-Daddy pride, feeling a tiny twinge of jealousy as the kids and their moms swarmed around my father—their Maestro—hoping for an autograph. Sometimes I'd be upset at having to share him with strangers, but once he caught my eye and waved, I knew I was the lucky one. I got to go home with him!

It wasn't long before my father's inspiring approach to reaching young audiences sparked the interest of orchestras around the country. Houston, Chicago, Buffalo, and Philadelphia all invited him to guest conduct not only concerts designed for children but programs for their adult patrons as well. He was constantly on the road, while also maintaining both his NBC and New Jersey Symphony schedules.

In 1954, after two seasons guest conducting children's concerts with the Philadelphia Orchestra, musical director Eugene Ormandy appointed Dad to be director of *all* their Young People's Concerts.

Ormandy wrote: "I am not exaggerating when I tell you that your performances were outstanding. . . . Your young audiences love you and every member of the orchestra talks about you with the highest regard. What more can I say to a colleague other than thank you and sincerest congratulations?"

However, Dad's most coveted invitation came from Toscanini himself. In a tremendous show of support and respect, the Maestro recommended that he guest conduct several NBC Symphony concerts. I doubt that any other honor could have held more meaning for my father.

In the following chapter, "A Visit with Toscanini," he describes another honor and coveted invitation. That visit in 1952 was a unique occasion. Although the Maestro often chatted with the players after rehearsals, it was rare to be invited to his home for a private discussion. My father recounts his visit to Toscanini's Riverdale, New York, estate, where he sought guidance from the Maestro for his biggest undertaking to date

Sam and Eugene Ormandy.

TUNE IN

SAMUEL ANTEK

Conductor, New Jersey Symphony

Conducts the

NBC SYMPHONY ORCHESTRA

NBC Coast-to-Coast

SAT., JUNE 28 • 6:30-7:30 P. M. (E.D.S.T.)

with the New Jersey Symphony: conducting Verdi's *Requiem*. Toscanini had conducted this magnificent piece many times and had his own musical history with the eminent composer. At nineteen, Toscanini had already been a cellist at Milan's Teatro alla Scala when Giuseppe Verdi supervised the premiere of his new opera, *Otello*. That initial association led to Toscanini's lifelong dedication to interpreting Verdi's works with the utmost accuracy.

In the comfort of Toscanini's study at Villa Pauline, which overlooked the Hudson River, these two musicians—two colleagues, two conductors, each passionate about his art—talked about how to interpret a composer's detailed markings. How to find the "pulse," the "sonority" within the indicated tempo. How loud is "forte"? How soft is "pianissimo"? How to discover what the composer intended—always Toscanini's particular objective. How to make beautiful music.

Chapter 4
A VISIT WITH TOSCANINI

AS A MEMBER OF the NBC Symphony for all its seventeen years, I had many opportunities to observe Toscanini on and off the podium. I also had many occasions to speak to him informally—during intermissions in a rehearsal, at various social events such as cocktail parties, etc., given intermittently by either Toscanini or the management, and at chance meetings when the Maestro attended rehearsals of other conductors at NBC.

At these informal encounters, Toscanini's first reaction was to peer intently at my face, as though to make sure who I was. No matter what anyone said to him, no matter how tired he might be, he was always immediately interested and would become absorbed in the conversation. Toscanini was always talkative, full of memories and associations. But it was difficult to have an extended conversation with him alone; invariably, others gathered around.

As I have said before, there was a curious impersonality about Toscanini. No one I have ever seen with him, including close friends and members of his family, seemed naturally intimate or at ease with him. It was always as if he were something apart, as if he were a separate island surrounded by a moat no one dared cross. This impression was emphasized even when I heard friends and persons who saw him daily speak to him.

I had often mentioned to Toscanini works that I was going to conduct with my New Jersey Symphony Orchestra, at times referring to a particular place in a composition to which I was interested in getting his reaction. One day I met him in the auditorium during an intermission in a rehearsal, and after the usual greeting, I said, "Maestro, I'm going to do the Verdi *Requiem* in New Jersey." His face lit up. "*Bene, bene*, beautiful, beautiful—eh! *Molto drammatico!*" By this time his hands were clenched and he was shaking them in the air to emphasize what he was saying. "That's a real 'Dies Irae,' eh? Not like that Mozart *Requiem!*" he snorted in disdain. "A 'Dies Irae' with one trombone!—hmph! . . . Must have good chorus too!" I told him I thought we would have a chorus of about a hundred. "Good, good—plenty! Verdi did not intend to have a chorus larger than one hundred twenty. You have good voices? Is difficult for sopranos, eh?" I told him I had engaged Herva Nelli as the soprano soloist. "Oh!" he said, "beautiful voice."

Though I had played the *Requiem* several times with Toscanini and felt I had absorbed the essentials of his wonderful approach to Verdi's works, I was quite anxious to speak to him at length about various details. It was impossible to do so at these chance encounters. However, I finally took courage and one day asked if I could possibly see him to discuss the work. "Sure, sure," he said. "Come up to Riverdale. Call me." An appointment was arranged with his secretary, and within the week I found myself at eleven o'clock one morning in the spacious formal living room of the Villa Pauline. I had been there only once before, at the reception he gave for the orchestra after our tour.

I was admitted by a houseboy who spoke practically no English, only Italian. On the wall was the striking pastel of Toscanini I had noticed on my previous visit. The boy asked me my name and disappeared, only to return in a few minutes. I was then told to go upstairs. A broad central staircase led up to a large balcony, off which were numerous rooms. As I came to the top of the stairs, Toscanini was waiting, dressed in a blue brocade dressing gown over maroon pajamas. I was unprepared for the informality, and it seemed to me that the Old Man looked rather tired. He greeted me warmly, however, and led me through a narrow hallway to his study, which adjoined his bedroom. Several windows looked out upon the garden sloping down to the Hudson in the distance. A piano was in one corner; a life-size bust of Verdi in another; a desk stood before the windows, and a large radio loudspeaker was against one wall. I was struck by the profusion of pictures and photographs in the room—the piano top was literally covered with photographs and mementos.

There were also a number of photographs of Toscanini in the house—all very handsome, flattering, dashing, and youthful looking. I was surprised by all this, remembering his shyness and his much publicized bouts with photographers. In his eighties, Toscanini would often comment on his age and, like everyone getting along in years, liked to hear it said that he wasn't "old" at all. True, while conducting he would scream, "I am young—you are old! Wake up!" but otherwise he seemed to enjoy being reassured.

As we entered the study, Toscanini seated me in a chair facing the piano and then sat down himself in the piano chair, turning it toward me. I had brought with me a long list of particular points in the *Requiem* that I wanted to go over with him and thought that I would immediately get down to business. However, as he seated himself, he began to talk rather apologetically about what had happened the night before. I knew there had been a special recording session with the NBC Symphony that I unfortunately had not been able to attend because of a commitment with my New Jersey Symphony. They were recording the Brahms Third. I gathered from what Toscanini was telling me that there had been a scene at the session and he had walked out after the usual imprecations. In vain he had been importuned to come back. As he was recounting the incident, he became completely absorbed, singing various parts of the Brahms, indicating the tempi with his hands. "Oh!" he said, "This is a difficult symphony—so hard to capture the spirit." I reminded him of the first time we had played it with him some dozen years before; how he had cried, "This is Italian music, not German music!" I remembered so vividly his dramatic singing of the weeping opening phrases in the strings. I did not mention, however, that the next time we played it, several years later, I had been almost shocked at the change in tempi and whole approach—everything seemed slower, more expansive and deliberate.

Verdi is to the left, Brahms to the right, and the open score is a Beethoven septet.

In talking about music with Toscanini, or, more accurately, when Toscanini was talking about his reactions to music, he continually emphasized his eternal quest for the "right" tempi, the "right" spirit, and his constant revaluation of his musical approach and ideas. As we talked about the first time we had played the Brahms Third, he began to wonder about the time we had most recently performed it and, not being able to remember the date, went to his desk, on which stood a big circular file. He began to search through it, this evidently being a record of his performances. He was annoyed to find that the Brahms was not even listed. The file was similar to those usually seen in offices and libraries, and I felt that Toscanini looked upon it as a new gadget or toy and was more hurt that it had failed him than that the specific information was missing. The file had not only the dates of performances of many works but the timings of the different performances. I was interested to see that here was proof positive of what I had always known: that the timings of various performances differed considerably and that the stories of Toscanini's timings being exactly the same at all performances of a particular work were so much nonsense. Through all this, of course, Toscanini kept up a constant flow of talk dealing with all phases of music and performance.

I was very eager to get on to the *Requiem*, but I did not want to break the Old Man's train of thought. "The correct tempi—that is the important thing—the right tempi! Oh, how difficult! But the sonority, too . . . *molto importante!*" He began to tell me that the previous week he had heard a radio performance of the Shostakovich Seventh Symphony, that he had pulled out the score and listened, that everything seemed right, that the tempi were *"giusti,"* but that it all had seemed boring, uninteresting. "And," he said, "I remembered when I conducted it that it is good piece—I couldn't understand." So he called up NBC and asked them to send him the record that had been made when he conducted it the first time and he said, with great simplicity, "Yes—it was 'different.'" He said it was all in the sonority, the breadth and thickness of the sound, the expressiveness within the tempo that gave the music true utterance . . . Tempo in itself was nothing, it had to have pulse, it changed always like your heartbeat. He held up his hand, and in the palm he traced a diagram to illustrate what he had been talking about. He drew a vertical line. This, he said, is the tempo, and then across, weaving in and out sinuously, he traced a wavy line, like a snake wrapped around a stick. "That," he said, "is the way the tempo must change—weaving in and out, but always close and always returning, never like this," drawing a line away from the original line, at a tangent. "Yes," he said, "in music, just to have the correct tempo without all that goes with it means nothing." I was interested to hear him putting into words what you felt so definitely when you played with him. So many conductors follow a certain metronome marking, because it is Toscanini's, without feeling the musical justification for it.

Metronome markings, whether his own or not, seemed to be a fetish with Toscanini. I have never seen a score that he used for any length of time that did not have his own metronome marking for each movement. He set great store, too, by the metronome markings the composer indicated. He would castigate a conductor who changed the markings of a composer, but at the same time, paradoxically, he would quite naïvely brush aside his own deviations. However, I should point out that these deviations, usually slight, were part of a complete musical logic and, above all, were fewer than those of perhaps any other conductor.

In connection with metronome markings, Toscanini mentioned the following incident. Shortly after a well-known conductor had conducted Schumann's Second Symphony, he met Toscanini and asked him how he had liked it. "I told him," said Toscanini, "it was bad—all too slow. I asked him, 'Why don't you follow Schumann's metronome markings?'" The conductor answered, "The markings are wrong—no good—they're too fast." To which Toscanini replied, almost gleefully, "I'd rather be wrong and close to Schumann than right and close to you!"

One must not assume, however, that Toscanini was slavish to the metronome markings of composers. In fact, it was always a bit disconcerting, after hearing a story such as this, to hear Toscanini talk about a section in the Beethoven Ninth and casually mention that a certain metronome marking was too fast, that in relation to the tempo that preceded it, it must be different from the one Beethoven indicated. As Toscanini often said, "In music, two times two makes five." There is no one, of course, in music making who hews exactly to the line; everyone makes his deviations, and rightly so, in the name of expressiveness. But Toscanini's deviations were the least of any conductor, as his own illustration of the weaving line indicates so aptly.

Toscanini's observations about the relationship between tempo and sonority were very interesting to me as an orchestral musician: a certain tempo will seem absolutely wrong if an awareness of volume, warmth, and intensity is lacking. On the other hand, with these qualities, the tempo seems right and justifiable. That is why the metronome markings Toscanini placed on a piece of music are only one of the many ingredients that made the true tempo indications "his." His tempo in the slow movement of the Haydn Symphony no. 88 illustrates this point. His actual tempo was much slower than that of many other conductors. The quarter-note melody movement is rather static, repetitious, and slow moving. It might seem that taking it faster would solve the musical problem. Not so with Toscanini. I remember how he insisted on taking a very slow, sustained tempo—one I believe would be deadly with almost anyone else. But with him, it became "correct." How he worked to have the cellos "sing" that melody; how warm he wanted the sound. "Is a prayer, a prayer!" he cried, bringing his hands up in a beseeching gesture, raising his face upward and almost bending his knees, singing in his cracked, raucous, bleating voice. "So! So! Put something—feel something—*accidenti!*" It was wonderful to hear and see how, under this stimulation, the melody truly sang its noble, unhurried way. Without this atmosphere, this inspiration, this sonority, the slow tempo would have been without meaning; it would have seemed endless, boring. It was in this kind of musical illumination that Toscanini's flame of genius burned brightest. Few other conductors could probe so deeply into the inner soul of the music.

I was often struck by certain little peculiarities in Toscanini's tempi in the overtures to operas seldom performed—certain holds and rubatos that were not indicated. I remember him once, in Weber's Overture to *Der Freischütz*, stopping the orchestra after he had insisted on inserting a slight fermata to tell us that that was the way the soprano sang it in the opera and that was the way it should be played. Toscanini often used to say that "we," that is, we modern instrumentalists, had lost the art of playing the old masters, that we had no feeling for their styles or their traditions.

I had been at Toscanini's home for at least an hour, and the subject I had come to discuss, the Verdi *Requiem*, had not yet been mentioned. I was concerned about taking up too much of his time, but Toscanini moved from one piece of music to another, singing a melody here and there, completely carried away in his absorption. It was a beautiful experience to just sit there and watch how his mind worked. He spoke a great deal about the Beethoven Ninth. We had played it at a concert two weeks before and had recorded it. Here again, in his concern about the tempi, he had studied the score for weeks before he conducted it. "Is so difficult!" He shook his head disparagingly, for he had never felt happy about any of his past performances of the work. "People come and tell me afterward how good it is. I listen to a record!" Then he added, sadly and plaintively, "Is terrible! Antek," he said almost apologetically, "I can only do my best. I try to be honest." He looked out toward the window and garden. "A man is like a tree, or a blade of grass—he can only do what he can."

Through all this talk, I had been holding my *Requiem* score in my hand. He must have noticed my fingering of the pages. "Ah, yes! The *Requiem*—what did you want to ask me? But," he said, "you know it, no? You played it with me many times." He took my score and began to leaf through the pages. "Remember! In Verdi—never too soft the piano—but *naturale!*" He recounted the story I had heard him tell before of his experience playing under Verdi, who was conducting his own opera, *Otello*. Toscanini had been the second cellist. In the last scene of act 1, there is a passage for four solo celli marked pianissimo, and, said Toscanini, "I played what I thought was a real pianissimo. During intermission," he went on, "I saw Verdi coming toward my stand. I was so frightened as this great man came toward me I could not move. Verdi said, 'Who plays the second cello?' 'I do,' I said." At this point Toscanini told with relish how his

Toscanini manuscript. Excerpt from solo quartet of Beethoven's Ninth Symphony.

partner had given him a push, bringing him to his feet, saying, "Ignoramus, when the great Verdi talks to you, stand up!" "Verdi told me, 'Don't play too soft—play stronger.' But I said to him, 'Maestro, you marked pianissimo.' 'Never mind,' said Verdi, 'it must be heard—play *naturale*.' You see," said Toscanini to me, "never too soft the piano in Italian music—is different from German music." The opening of *Aida*, for instance, is a very good example of what Toscanini meant. It is marked "ppp" (pianissimo), but when we did it, we played what any other conductor would have called "mf" (mezzo forte). We played our instruments with a singing, natural sound, with the normal weight of the bow, with neither exaggerated lightening of the stick nor ticklish concern for a gossamer delicacy.

The Old Man fingered through the score, pointing out certain phrases, certain places in the orchestration: for example, the clarinet and bassoon passages in the "Dies Irae." "It is never heard, never! Make sure they play forte!" (It is marked pianissimo in the score.) He stopped suddenly, looked up with furrowed brow as though trying to remember something. "I add something somewhere here—I double something. I remember—the flute, I think." He looked through the score, could not seem to find it, and went on to something else. (I remembered the particular section and, later, when I went home, I looked through it very carefully trying to find the exact spot. I thought I found it and next time I saw him, I called his attention to it.) He finally came to a place just before the "Lacrimosa" that had been particularly puzzling to me. My score was a miniature. In rehearsing with my orchestra, I had found that the orchestra parts differed in some details from the score I had. The first violin part had a trill over the E flat just before the largo section, but this was not in the score. "Which is right?" I asked him. He looked at the place, puckered his brows, pursed his lips. "I think . . . no . . . no trill. I used to . . . once . . . play with a trill, but it seemed clumsy—not natural. I don't think Verdi wrote the trill—but wait, we shall see. Where is my score?"

We got up and walked to the little hallway adjoining his study. Along the walls were shelves filled with large orchestral scores. He began to look through the shelves.

I, too, began to search—it was not there, it seemed. I found a small piano score. "No," he said, "not that—a big one." He was becoming exasperated. I said, "Maestro, I don't want to take your time over this." "No, no," he said, "the score is here somewhere. I know—*Walter, Walter,*" he began to bellow. In a few moments, Walter came running up and joined in the search. We finally found the full-size conductor's score, bound in white calfskin, on a lower shelf. The Old Man pulled it off the shelf and began to carry it to the desk, brushing aside our offers to help him.

Walter left, and the Old Man opened the score. "You see," he said with pride, "it is the copy of the original manuscript in Verdi's own writing." He pointed to the dedication, to a Madame Stolz. He made a point of telling me that she was a singer who had been Verdi's mistress after his wife died. He leafed through the delicately written score until he came to the place in question and bent over until his nose almost touched it. There *was* a trill in Verdi's own writing over the note in the violin part. He stared at it. "Hmph!" he said. "I think is a mistake. I think Verdi meant a tenuto." It was obviously a trill, however. "No, no trill," said the Old Man. "I think is better without trill." I could not help but smile inwardly at the very typical Toscanini paradox. The man who screamed at us, "Play what's written! Verdi always wrote what he wanted!" blithely decided, Verdi notwithstanding, no trill! Such heresy, I thought. What would all the Toscanini devotees who had lovingly built up their stories of his idolatrous worship of the printed note say to this?

Toscanini often indulged in these personal-taste reactions to small details: changing, coming back to the original, changing again. I had the feeling as he peered at this particular spot in the Verdi score that he was rather taken aback by actually finding the trill there after having played it otherwise, and I could almost visualize him when he conducted the work again, saying so typically to the orchestra, "Let's try it with a trill," listening, and then, "I think is better—play with trill. I think I am stupid, no? Verdi knew what he wanted, no? I get old—sometimes I do stupid things." There were many such instances in Toscanini's career which seemed to reflect his concern with always finding a fresh approach, his willingness to change, to reverse himself. This often left his overly worshipful disciples in embarrassing positions.

Time was moving along, and again I felt I was overstaying my welcome. I mentioned once more that I did not want to abuse his kindness. "No," he said, "not at all. Wait—" and off he was again, looking through the score. It seemed almost sacrilegious to break into his thoughts with any of the specific minutiae I had in mind. "Such a beautiful melody," he would say, as he sang and silently conducted each new section. Suddenly he was off on a tangent again, talking about Dimitri Mitropoulos and the modern music he played so much—as though the beautiful melodies of Verdi brought to mind the transgressions of modern dissonance. "Why does Mitropoulos conduct that terrible music—such noise—why, if I were playing the cello under his nose he wouldn't know what I was playing. No!" snorted the Old Man. "I couldn't learn twenty bars of that—is not music!" There were other suggestions about the Verdi score. Then he asked about my New Jersey Symphony, how many members there were, how big the hall was. I had a feeling he would have been interested in coming to a rehearsal of the concert, but I felt I could not take advantage of him. I also knew that were he to come, the chorus, the soloists, and the orchestra, including myself, would have been petrified.

Finally, I again indicated that I should be leaving, and the Old Man walked with me to the door of his study. I mentioned how much I and all the orchestra were looking forward to his return. He smiled rather sadly and shook his head. "How I suffer when I conduct," he said. "I am never happy with myself—never." He suddenly turned toward me and took both my hands in his. "My dear Antek," he said, "I am always so nervous when I have to step before the orchestra—even after all these years—it is as though the first time I conduct!"

I looked at him almost incredulously. "Maestro—no, I can't believe it!"

"Yes! Yes!" he said rather forlornly. I cast discretion aside, put my arms around his shoulders, and hugged him warmly, as though to express how deeply we all loved him. Our Old Man nervous before *us!* The idea!

At the head of the stairs, he shook hands with me, and I left him. Once outside, I rather dazedly walked up the street with the feeling that the past hours had been a dream. What a privilege it was to have had Maestro completely to myself for two hours. My visit had not revealed anything essentially new or different; it merely emphasized and underlined the qualities and characteristics of which I was already aware. What was particularly fascinating and pleasing to me was that he had, for the first time, expressed verbally his fundamental attitude toward music, an attitude I had only conjectured about or interpreted before. It gave me a strong feeling of truly understanding Toscanini and the things for which he was striving. Above all, it was a complete affirmation of how he loved music: it seemed to envelop him completely. Music, its problems, its fulfillment, its smallest details, were the beginning and end of everything.

I do not flatter myself that what he said or how he reacted that morning was inspired in any way by me personally. Almost any sympathetic person sitting there would have called forth the same stream-of-consciousness soliloquizing on the part of the Old Man. You might interject a word or a thought; he would tolerate the interruptions, look at you with piercing eyes for a moment, and be off again on a different tangent, complete with dramatic gestures—singing, conducting, or snorting his disdain.

What struck me, too, during this extended visit was that at no time did Toscanini give the impression that he was talking to anyone but an equal. There was no feeling that he was "teaching" me, no feeling of condescension—that he was the "Maestro" and I just a member of the orchestra. While looking over the Verdi score on the desk, he was as interested and eager as a child. A vivid feeling of rediscovery welled up in him, and in talking to me he seemed to be talking to himself.

When I left the house that afternoon, I did not know that within the next two weeks I would be seeing Toscanini again at his home. A few days after my visit, all of us in the NBC Symphony were invited with our wives to the Villa Pauline for cocktails and a buffet supper—a sort of "goodbye" at the end of the season. This party was more or less a duplication of the one given after our tour, with many of the same people present—the orchestra, some close friends, and officials of NBC. It was a typically sumptuous affair, with champagne, liquors, and heaping trays of delicious hors d'oeuvres beautifully served.

The evening proved a particularly memorable one for me. Many persons had already arrived and spread themselves in small groups throughout the long living room and on the spacious outdoor stone balcony overlooking the garden. Toscanini was at one end of the balcony, surrounded by several members of the orchestra, and my wife and I went over to pay our respects. As we approached, I noted that the Old Man seemed to be looking his best. As always, he was impeccably dressed, in a gray suit, starched collar, bow tie, and highly polished shoes. His face was shining, and he looked well and handsome—so much better than he had the morning I visited him several days before.

"Hello, Maestro," I greeted him. He peered at me for an instant; then, "Ah! Antek!" he said in a particularly effusive manner, taking my hand in both of his and shaking it warmly. I was rather startled, for he had never greeted me in such a personal way. "Ah, Antek!" he continued, patting my arm, smiling. "I read your article about me. You know, no one shows me anything. I didn't see the program until last night. De Vecchi showed it to me." He was referring to the program of our performance of the Beethoven Ninth that had taken place about two weeks before. My article, "Playing with the Maestro," had been reprinted in it. This article had originally appeared in print two years earlier on the eve of our national tour. Several times in the past, we had had occasion to speak of it, and he usually parried my question as to whether he had read it by saying how much he hated to read about himself. He did tell me once, in referring to the article, however, that people told him it was "good," and added earnestly, "But you know me—so? You played with me—no?"

I was so pleased by this belated recognition of the article that I took his hand and said, rather anxiously, "Maestro, you don't mind the things I told, do you?" He smiled affably, in a wonderfully expansive manner. *"Bene, bene,"* he said. "Many things you understand—no? But, you know, I couldn't finish it. To read about myself"—he waved his hand in that typical self-deprecatory way—"is so difficult for me!" He patted my hand, and I could see he was quite pleased and touched. We left him to make room for others who were coming up to greet him. A few moments later, I turned, and there was Toscanini, our eighty-four-year-old Maestro, standing on the stone terrace, smiling and chatting animatedly with those around him.

I should mention how amazing the Old Man's endurance was at the party. In the course of the evening, he greeted several hundred guests personally and chatted with them all. Though he was constantly surrounded by groups of people, he was always most charming and vivacious in both manner and speech. When we left after several hours, he seemed as fresh and vibrant as when we arrived. The party lasted quite a while longer, and Toscanini, I was later told, kept going until the end.

It was interesting and also typical that all the guests were greeted and spoken to with the same warmth. The player sitting at the last stand, the concertmaster, General Robert Sarnoff—all seemed to be the same; there were no "favorites." How warmly he would talk with members of the orchestra whom a few days before, at a rehearsal, he had been vilifying and castigating! He was enthusiastically interested in what anyone said, and any question put to him usually started him off on a stream of reminiscences. Our Old Man truly loved us all.

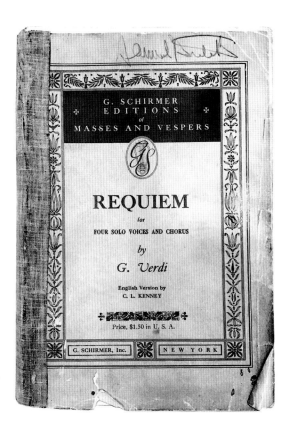

Postscript from Lucy Antek Johnson:

I would like to think that Dad's conversation with the Maestro about Verdi's *Requiem*—especially regarding the imperative to remain faithful to the composer's intentions—had a most positive effect on the performance of the New Jersey Symphony. The *New York Times* agreed:

> *The orchestra was rich in sound, responsive to Mr. Antek's wishes. . . . It had the overall effect that Verdi intended—the brooding darkness, fiery outbursts, the passages of mysterious quietness and the soaring grandeur.*

—*The New York Times*, April 29, 1952

1947 - 1957

**MUSICAL DIRECTOR
NEW JERSEY SYMPHONY**

AND

GUEST CONDUCTOR

WITH

N.-B.-C. SYMPHONY — NEW YORK

PHILADELPHIA ORCHESTRA

HOUSTON SYMPHONY ORCH.

BUFFALO PHILHARMONIC ORCH.

ROCHESTER CIVIC ORCH.

and others

SAMUEL **ANTEK**
CONDUCTOR

TOSCANINI CONDUCTS OBERON

BY HIS EARLY FORTIES, my father had become quite the glamorous and celebrated musical personality. The combination of playing with Toscanini and achieving success as a conductor had brought Dad an abundance of attention. He was now formally addressed as *Dr.* Samuel Antek (having received an honorary doctorate from his alma mater, Chicago Musical College), and his picture was often in the paper after one of his spirited New Jersey concerts. He was invited to contribute more articles to newspapers and magazines, he was sought after for radio interviews, and, most significantly, he was commissioned to write this book.

Everyone wanted to know: "Was Toscanini really that good? Was he really that temperamental? How did it feel to play with him?" The phone never stopped ringing. My father was famous! Not that I was old enough to fully understand what that meant. Yes, I knew Dad was busier. Yes, he traveled more. Yes, he had to juggle his expanding schedule. And yes, my mother and I had to adjust to the shifts in our routine. But our family time was sacred and savored, whether it was spending summers in the Berkshires or building snowmen on West Seventy-Sixth Street in the winters.

Dad had two favorite ways to relax, and I don't know which he relished more: playing a vigorous game of tennis—he was known for his powerful serve—or watching a Dodgers game and cheering along with the stadium crowd when Jackie Robinson stole home base.

Favorites for us all were the Sunday evenings when various string players from the NBC Symphony gathered at our house to play chamber music. Those get-togethers were so informal that my mother, the only nonpro in the group, was often invited to accompany them on piano. As I recall, she kept up pretty well. Already tucked away in my bed for the night, I could hear the mellow sounds coming from down the hall, along with bursts of laughter whenever someone shared a new joke or the latest musical gossip.

But the times my Dad and I spent alone together were the most precious. He loved to entertain me with stories about his childhood in Chicago. "The snow was *how* high?" I'd ask in wonder. Sometimes he would waltz me around the room as I stood on top of his shoes, letting me pretend that I was a prima ballerina. I also recall his utter joy when he dove into a bowl of one of my mother's culinary specialties, her mushroom and barley soup. With marrowbones! "Alice," he'd exclaim, "this was the best one you've ever made!" He said that every time.

When I reread his next chapter, which examines Toscanini's interpretation of one particular work, Carl Maria von Weber's *Oberon* Overture, I was reminded of another precious memory. One afternoon, when I was about eight, I stood outside the closed doors of the living room, listening to my father at the piano. He had been there for hours. First he'd play a series of notes, then a chord, then another few notes, and then there would be a pause as he penciled in notations on the many sheets of music. Then he'd hum something, and then he'd play another chord. This didn't sound like his usual practicing. It didn't even sound like music to me. I didn't dare disturb him, but I was curious. What was he doing? Summoning up my courage, I opened the door as quietly as I could. Instead of shooing me away, he smiled and motioned me in to sit next to him on the narrow piano bench so he could show me what he was working on. He explained that he was preparing an orchestral score for an upcoming concert in New Jersey. The orchestra would be performing Mendelssohn's Symphony no. 4, also known as the *Italian* symphony.

At that point, I had been taking piano lessons for more than a year, but my sheet music didn't look like that! I was dazzled by the many folded music pages spread out across the piano, with the different sections designating horns, strings, woodwinds, percussion, and chorus. I was particularly impressed when Dad said he could hear it coming together in his head as he worked through the phrasing. That was my first introduction to the complexity of a symphonic score.

In his next chapter, he guides the reader on a bar-by-bar journey through the score of Toscanini's meticulous and distinctive approach to Weber's *Oberon* Overture. He illustrates, from both a player's and a conductor's perspective, all the creative choices Toscanini made over many years of rehearsals and performances. We learn how much time and effort went into striking just the right tone for each note, each bar, and each instrument's part.

Music critic Edward Downes, in his *New York Times* review of the book, called the *Oberon* chapter "perhaps the most fascinating chapter of the entire book."

It certainly is a departure from the previous chapters. It is an essay written by a musician for musicians. It is more scholarly, with a musical vocabulary unfamiliar to most readers. Dotted eighth? Fermata? Sforzando? One may not know those terms, but one doesn't have to be a musician to appreciate the fervor, the players' shared passion of discovery, the nuances, and the intriguing anecdotes my father tells about the hours of dedication it took to achieve the Maestro's unique vision.

That vision was equally admired by other conductors. When asked what made Toscanini's conducting so special, conductor Eugene Ormandy said: "He played every instrument with his baton. He had meaning from beat to beat. It wasn't just one-two-three-four; it was what happened between one and two, between two and three. . . . I've never seen that before."

After reading my father's words, I hope you will listen to a recording of the NBC Symphony playing the *Oberon* Overture and pay close attention to the opening horn solo and the subtle entrance of the strings. You will be rewarded with a renewed appreciation of what it took to achieve that inspired sound.

Samuel Antek's original first-draft
handwritten page of this chapter.

Chapter 5

TOSCANINI CONDUCTS OBERON

I WILL TRY TO bring Toscanini's many and varied qualities as conductor and musician more sharply into focus by taking you through a complete work at rehearsal, giving you, as it were, a blow-by-blow description of what went on with regard to both Toscanini himself and his effect on the playing of the musicians in the orchestra. I have chosen Weber's Overture to *Oberon* because of its great familiarity both to audiences and players and because it affords an opportunity to describe some of the salient features of the "Toscanini approach."

Oddly enough, though we had not played this overture with Toscanini more than six times in seventeen years, his approach to it remains vividly in my mind. We had, of course, played it many times during that period with any number of other conductors, both obscure and famous. But what is of greatest interest to me in looking back at the various rehearsals and performances with Toscanini is the variety of approaches and emphases he made use of each time we played the work. I shall telescope all these rehearsals into a continuous picture.

Whenever *Oberon* was scheduled for rehearsal, the Old Man would turn to us in his usual manner and announce in that laconic, gruff voice, "Weber," or perhaps *"Oberon,"* with no other word or gesture to the players. He never looked at the first horn to see if he was ready for his very difficult opening solo but would remain silent, his face somber, his head forward. In this forbidding, formless atmosphere, he would start an almost imperceptible upbeat that moved no more than an inch or two. In this breathless

vacuum, the sound of the horn seemed like an apparition—no cue, no indication of any sort had been given to the player. Toscanini would beat a very slow, tenuous beat of four through the horn solo. It seemed as if the bar would never end, as if it were lost in space, and we in the strings seemed scarcely to breathe as we silently prepared for our entrance in the second bar (first and second violins).

His gesture in that opening bar, with an undulating, sinuous movement, covered an area of but a few inches. A wonderful eerie, magical atmosphere was created in seconds; the mood for the whole introduction was set. The sound of the horn died out. Toscanini did not give any special cue for the horn to finish as it held the fermata at the end of the bar; it was as though he waited for the sound to die out naturally. Again would come that same slow upbeat as at the beginning, hardly moving, an almost imperceptible glance or direction to the violins, and we would start to play. The lack of cue or beat made it particularly difficult for us to play the first sixteenth note together with the second violins, which had the same rhythmic figure we did.

On the face of it, it would seem simple for even an average performer, let alone for the expert musicians of the NBC Symphony, to play two notes in basic dotted eighth and sixteenth rhythm, but the fact remains that it is one of the most difficult ensemble feats for even a virtuoso orchestra to perform when, in a very slow, dragging tempo, Toscanini insisted on conducting in a slow-motion beat of four to the bar, without subdividing into eighths. Sitting in the orchestra, I

often got the feeling in such places of being in a slowly skidding car with nothing to hold on to. Worried, you look to the conductor for the needed helpful direction or hint. The problem is your own; you must place that sixteenth note in exactly its proper place and in the exact time relationship to the whole drawn out beat. It is amazing how different are the conceptions of even the most experienced group of players as to the value of a sixteenth note in a very slow tempo.

It would have helped greatly, of course, if Toscanini had indicated the basic tempo very positively, but that would have affected the mood completely. You must remember that Toscanini was conducting with small, formless, undulating beats from the very beginning—even the upbeat to the strings in the second bar when they started was not indicated by any obvious motion or accent. You were truly on your own, with your eye, your ear, and every musical instinct alert, ready to fit yourself into the ensemble. The first time we would play this entrance for the strings, it would never be right; the sixteenth note was always ragged. Toscanini's reactions on such occasions varied. In an ominous, rumbling grumble, with rising, threatening cadence, he would mutter, "To-gether! To-ge-ther!"—the syllables pronounced in the rhythm of the slow tempo of the bar we were playing. "*T-o-g-e-t-h-e-r! T-o-g-e-t-h-e-r!*" with clenched jaw, and then, abruptly, "No! No! *DA CAPO! D-a—c-a-p-o!*" giving a menacing glance at the whole orchestra. We would start again with the horn solo at the very beginning. He might repeat exactly the motions I described earlier, and again we would come to the second-bar entrance of the violins. The strings, now well prepared for the problem, might sail past the reef without further mishap, although, playing, we would still not be certain of ourselves. The celli, too, had problems with their first entrance—an unaccented sixteenth note without any subdivided beat from Toscanini. Looking over at them, I would see their strained, watchful eyes.

At other times, should the bar of the string entrance still not be right, the tension would mount, and a full-blown "Toscanini flare-up" might occur, with "*Vergognas!*" flying and a stream of abuse at musicians who were so stupid and illiterate that we couldn't play one even sixteenth within a beat! Often he would beat out each sixteenth note of the quarter note by violently slapping his baton on the stand—"One—two—three," and then, with special emphasis, "four!"—screaming raucously, "*Lunghe note! LU-N-GHE note!* (Long notes!) You eat the notes! *Lunghe note!*" By this time, in the excitement and furor, he was emphasizing and conducting each eighth note as against the original beat of slow four. This, of course, wholly simplified the problem, and, as my partner once whispered to me, "Why didn't he do that right at the beginning instead of going nuts?" But this "going nuts" was typical of Toscanini. This insistence in slow movements of beating the broadest possible quarter notes without subdivisions is one of the most difficult feats and achievements of the truly virtuoso conductor; this very subtle, musical blending of mood and beat is something few conductors are capable of and most, unfortunately, never even seek.

We usually think of virtuoso baton technique in a more spectacular sense, such as beating complicated rhythms, giving very sure, positive entrances, and managing sudden changes of tempo. These are, in a sense, the more obvious conductorial appurtenances.

What Toscanini sought was something much rarer, something beyond the rules and textbook formulas. No other conductor I know of (with the possible exception of Mitropoulos) would even have asked the orchestra to play the opening of *Oberon* in so broad and slow a beat of four. Without exception, they would subdivide into eighths— some more obviously, some very subtly. No one else even sought or attempted to seek Toscanini's vision. I say "sought" for even the Maestro did not completely reach his goal. Often at a concert, in spite of having insisted that he would never "insult" himself and the orchestra by subdividing, he relented almost unconsciously as the ensemble rocked and would give the most subtle little indications of tempo change. In other words, he would do what was logical and safe. I have often asked myself on such occasions why Toscanini hadn't used the technically safe approach in the first place and thus saved himself, the orchestra, and everyone concerned so much aggravation and heartache. But even as I asked the question, I knew the answer—Toscanini never sought, nor did he even seem aware of, the easy, practical, safe approach to conducting and music making.

I have used both the terms "conducting" and "music making," but perhaps I should more correctly call it just "music making," for Toscanini's physical motions in conducting stemmed completely from the musical thought, the mood, and emotion. I was seldom, if ever, aware of a conducting formula or the application of a technical conducting device. We would often sweat blood over what to any other conductor was child's play as far as any "beating" problem or ensemble difficulty was concerned.

I have spoken of the extraordinary mood Toscanini achieved in the few opening bars of *Oberon*—the eerie, languorous, sylvan stillness, the quiet of nature that seems to roar in your ears with its silence; Toscanini conducting with his minimum of movement; the absolute sparseness of beat (in slow four), the utter lack of accent, direction, and cue; the slow, weighted beat like spiraling incense; and the intense absorption of the players, who were literally forced and goaded because of the difficulty of execution and the concentration and demands made on them under these circumstances. All this created an intangible tension, a feeling of silence that could be cut with a knife.

This fourth-dimensional pianissimo and quietude seldom has been achieved by other conductors, perhaps because of all their "correct" and more easily achieved technical address. Other conductors can tell you in a very definite, clear-cut manner what to do, but with Toscanini, because of the very expressive and potent, even purposeful, ambiguity of his direction, you found that *you* had to take most of the responsibility yourself. As a member of the orchestra, you were not only being "played upon"; you were performing with a care and selectivity of expression you seldom encounter in the course of orchestra playing. You had a personal stake in the mood you were creating; that intangible quality in your playing that you reserved for something you personally felt and wanted to express was forced to the surface. This can never happen when you are told what to do, when the problem is solved for you in advance. Most conductors, with all their cajolery, humorous efforts, tirades, sarcasm, kindness, or personal approach in dealing with an orchestra, can seldom reach below the surface of a player's capabilities. Not that the player is consciously aware of this; he would sincerely and indignantly deny he was resisting in any way. With Toscanini, you found you had a special gear shift you never knew existed, which suddenly gave you the power and strength you never thought was within you. Such is that phenomenon of response Toscanini inspired, exhorted, and, if necessary, drew out by force.

Another musical example, so similar in atmosphere to the opening of the *Oberon*, that expresses even more of Toscanini's attitude toward mood and beat is the opening of Strauss's *Death and Transfiguration*. This entrance is always difficult for an orchestra, starting as it does very softly and slowly in the violins and violas on an eighth-note rest—the next eighth note slurs into the following beat, which is a triplet, and so on. This again, as in the *Oberon*, presents a tricky ensemble problem for both player and conductor. I have played this work with several of the world's famous conductors—Walter, Reiner, Monteux, and others—and each one addresses himself almost completely and

immediately to the mechanics of seeing that the orchestra is absolutely precise in the placing and pacing of the eighth-note rest and the eighth note following. Each may warn the orchestra in advance of the difficulty; each, in his own way, whatever the upbeat he may give, will throw a hard, pointed, flicked, accented downbeat (the eighth note rest) in order to ensure as definitely as possible that the orchestra will come in positively on the first eighth note. Some will even subdivide this first downbeat into two parts, trying to doubly ensure the ensemble. Each beat of the bar will be flicked and accented so that the orchestra definitely achieves the ensemble whenever there is a tied note. The conductor will also ask the orchestra to play as softly as possible. He may speak of the mood he wants to achieve; he may counsel the orchestra against accents (although he will be making accents himself). With a first-class orchestra, the problem is usually overcome in a few moments, and the piece is launched and on its way. The problem has been solved.

As far as the audience is concerned, they hear an ephemeral pianissimo played in perfect ensemble. What else can one ask for? Nothing, it would seem. But, as far as we in the orchestra are concerned, everything! The problem was solved—but what of the "music"? Where was the inspiration not only for the ear of the listener but for us, the players? Where was the "true" conductorial art that conceals art? We musicians were in a sense made to feel impersonal. We responded as skilled artisans, not as inspired artists. Where was the glow and inspiration of mood, of music? Was the desired mood of death compatible with a conductor flicking precise, accented beats at us, his only concern seemingly that we produce perfect ensemble?

How different was the feeling and response built up within us by Toscanini's approach—his slow, small, curling, weighted, dragging, meditative upbeat followed by a downbeat immeasurably precise but without emphasis, without accent or expression! Toscanini stood severe, rapt, face unperturbed; the orchestra became suddenly immobile, and all around was the stillness of a tomb. In this airless, deathlike void, with greatest concentration and subtlest skill, we would seek to insinuate the opening eighth note.

All of us—we, Toscanini, the music—seemed welded together; we played, we felt, we held our breaths as though walking in a minefield. We were not just "playing"—this was not only a succession of beautifully sounded eighth notes or triplets formed into a particular pattern. Every note, held in the inexorable vise of the Old Man's slow, sinuous beat, seemed freighted with imponderable gloom, and we, together with Toscanini, were creating this mood, this atmosphere. We were not just standing by, fitting soft notes into proper patterns; we were "artists," each adding his daub of paint to a portrait of death: Toscanini, so austere and patrician, with his hands, his whole body and face, pantomiming the scene, we, with our bows and instruments, all joining in this ghostly pavane. This was music making at its highest consecrated level. How difficult it was to achieve, but what artistic satisfaction, what personal pride in so subtle and expressive an accomplishment. This was the realm of Toscanini's magic that only a player could plumb.

I will say with complete candor that some of the members of the orchestra did not approve of or completely understand what Toscanini was trying to do. Some looked upon these demands as idiosyncrasies, exaggerations, and many insisted that he just couldn't conduct, that he lacked "technique." They would triumphantly point to the performance of some guest conductor in a piece such as *Death and Transfiguration*, saying, "See how easy it is if it's conducted properly"—meaning mechanically correct. Some musicians tend, or perhaps I should say pretend, to be "hard boiled." They detested this "Toscanini fancy stuff"—to them, "a beat is a beat." The subtlety of a conductor who might purposely obscure his beat, the better to achieve a foggy, murky light, was beyond them. However, I think that in trying to fathom and probe this area of the unseen, this vague, emotional contact felt when playing with Toscanini, the most significant key will be found in the tremendous inspirational hold Toscanini had on those who played with him. For me, it dwarfed all his great, more obvious, and more dramatically publicized talents and gifts.

I have digressed, and we are on the opening bars of *Oberon*, but perhaps it is only through these seeming digressions that the working picture can be drawn. As we approached the first entrance of the flutes and clarinets in the sixth bar, I always watched very carefully to see what the Old Man would do and how the woodwinds would react to their difficult entrance. As with the horn in the opening bar, he rarely gave them any cue as they got set to breathe. Invariably, at a first rehearsal, the passage "sputtered" unevenly, the problem of ensemble the same in the winds as in the strings. The Old Man would glower. "To-ge-ther—to-ge-ther!"

Another conductor might begin to conduct the bar in eighths, prepare the woodwinds with a flicking, unobtrusive little upbeat, and would by this time very definitely have corralled the flutes and clarinets into a feeling of contact by a glance to bring them in with precision and confidence. This generally accepted conductorial approach was used in essential detail by every conductor except Toscanini. The players, as far as they were concerned, unquestionably liked the average, capable conductor's approach; it helped them. Players in an orchestra welcome a sympathetic glance or blink of an eye by a conductor, a reassuring little upbeat that steadies the tempo as they purse their lips. For the wind players, these aids are of particular meaning and importance. They are not left alone to find that split-second moment to start. It is difficult enough to begin alone; it becomes even more so when several players have to start together and are unable to see one another. It is in moments like these that the player looks up hopefully at the conductor, waiting and preparing himself for that helpful cue.

Alas, with Toscanini, the player looked in vain. At that difficult moment, needing every bit of help, he instead found himself alone, straining every faculty, instinct, and skill to bring himself in together with his colleagues. Players often told me how agonizing and nerve-racking an experience such moments were for them, especially when the only reward they got for their unsuccessful efforts was a "*Vergogna!*" or a searing, abusive tirade of invective and insult: "Babies! Children! *Dilettanti!* Not musicians you are! Cannot play a beat by yourselves! *Vergogna!* Am I a policeman to stand over you and beat? Play together!"

At the concert, I always had the feeling that the players crossed their fingers for luck and "jumped." Sometimes it came through perfectly, sometimes not.

In the slumberous, misty darkness of the opening, the scampering, cascading passage of the flutes and clarinets suddenly intrudes like a pale beam of moonlight. These passages are completely antithetical in musical relationship to the slow, muted harmonic background of the strings.

Sometimes, after bars such as I have been describing had been gone over several times, after Toscanini had chided and cajoled, the difference in sound and mood was something that would cause even the men to look at one another with almost grudging disbelief. Frequently, after such a moment, Toscanini would turn to the orchestra and say, "You see? You hear? This is music—no? Is something, eh? Is not the stupid notes but *musica!* You put something in the stupid notes, eh? *Corpo del vostro Dio!*"

Occasionally, in the seventh bar of the introduction, just before the second group of thirty-second notes in the woodwinds, Toscanini would call the players' attention to the fact that the solo horn had a sixteenth note just before they came in. He would caution them to wait for the horn, to take their time before starting so they could hear that sixteenth note clearly enunciated. He would caution the horn in turn to make the sixteenth long, broad. "Don't eat the note," he would say smilingly. "Take time, take time. Woodwinds wait for the horn!" Throughout this whole nine-bar introduction, he would warn the players to play as softly as possible. Toscanini's tempo in general was slower than was usual, but it often fluctuated at different rehearsals and between rehearsals and concerts. The differences were slight but unmistakable, with the tempo of the performance somewhat faster.

The tempo, slow as it was, however, was never static. I could feel that typical Toscanini plasticity. The beating of the stick seemed to follow along with the thought rather than merely indicate the arithmetical time in advance.

This peculiarly "sticky" beat was a phenomenon uniquely characteristic of Toscanini. Every conductor, of course, has his own characteristic type of beat. It is as personal as handwriting or a fingerprint. Each has his own mannerism, his own idiosyncrasy, his personal, effective dramatic and colorful gestures. Of all conductors I know, with the exception of perhaps Monteux, Toscanini's actual beating strokes were the least exaggerated or affected. One was never conscious of a stick trick. It was classic in its lack of ostentation and in its basic, simple modesty.

Toscanini himself often used the words "long," "sustained," "dragging," "holding," and "singing" to describe the effect he wanted with his baton movement. Another conductor might use these same words and phrases to describe a sustained sound, but only Toscanini would actually express their meaning through his slow-motion beat, through his whole conducting apparatus.

And now we arrive at Letter A—the tenth bar of the introduction. This is the very difficult entrance for the trumpets, horns, and bassoons, all of which, except the first horn, are playing now for the first time. Again Toscanini would hardly even glance at the players; again that slow, treacherous, unaccented upbeat, so very difficult to perform. The tempo here was still very slow, but imperceptibly it became a little more moving. This was quite different from the work of any other conductor, who invariably would do this section more brightly, more like a fanfare, and very definitely in a subdivided eight to the bar, or, if the tempo were faster, would conduct in an accented four to the bar.

Toscanini maintained the essential mood of the very opening, still distant and eerie.

At one rehearsal, just after the first bar of this section had been played, Toscanini stopped with an air of uncertainty. "The balance . . . I hear the trumpet but is not clear . . . The bassoon . . . bassoons! Don't play too soft . . . If I don't hear you, is nothing, eh?" Sometimes in such a place he would shrug his shoulders, smile, and say, "A stupid melody, maybe, but try to play as if it is a beautiful melody, no? . . . Sometimes we must try, even if is nothing . . . We put something, no? . . . Bassoon . . . a little louder!" They played the bar again, with the bassoons, the bass of the phrase, as it were, playing a

little more strongly, more accurately. The whole sound of the bar changed. To me, who had been playing in the orchestra through so many performances, it was suddenly as if I were hearing it for the first time. No one, before or since, had ever remarked upon the relationship between the trumpets and bassoons. It was always the trumpets that were heard; the rest of the instruments remained a murky, soft mass of sound. For the first time I heard clearly the counterpoint, the highlight of the bassoons, a strand of melody completely obscured before. I felt the delight of a boy who unexpectedly finds, to his joy, that there is an unseen second layer of chocolates concealed beneath the first!

In the next bar, too, Toscanini called attention to the flutes and clarinets—that even though they play only harmony notes, these must be played a little louder, the eighth note a little longer. With those stronger daubs of color, the whole bar suddenly sounded richer, more resonant, softer but with greater depth. In this bar, also, Toscanini would caution the first violins not to rush their groups of thirty-second notes: "*Uguale . . .* Don't rush." Sometimes he merely indicated this quality by dragging his beat even more, although at this point he tended almost to subdivide the beat. "*Uguale,*" he would softly counsel, his baton arm and his left hand dropping and straightening a bit, as if to stop our hurrying.

The fifth bar after A (bar 14) was played rather fully, "mp" or "mf," still in a broad, restrained tempo. Then, in the next bar, we would taper off with a diminuendo but without a ritard. A ritard was usually made here by other conductors, whose faster tempo had already brought them to the trumpet entrance and who had to compensate for it. Since Toscanini's tempo was already slow, there was no need for him to change. It must be borne in mind that, in these few bars starting with Letter A, a slowing, hardly discernible subdivision of beat would be made, not on each beat but instead with the slightest pulsation—still in the slow four to the bar.

In these seventh and eighth bars after Letter A, with the melody in a divisi of celli, Toscanini would always maintain a softness and distance, without the usually exaggerated dynamic of crescendo and diminuendo between the bars. Here, too, he would achieve a wonderful balance, cautioning the strings to continue playing very softly but indicating that the clarinets were to play more strongly. Every other conductor concentrated on the melody in the celli and violas; only Toscanini called attention to the role the clarinets were playing as part of the quartet. Only with Toscanini were they brought into happy perspective and balance, were they heard clearly. What had already seemed quite beautiful and clear suddenly became even more deliciously flavored; formless shadows here and there suddenly had outline and shape.

The last few remaining bars of the introduction were kept slow, soft, crawling. The bar just preceding the short fortissimo "tutti" chord, which is the "held" divisi of the violas alone, was stretched to its longest, held almost as though there were a fermata at the end, although Toscanini beat out the whole bar in slow, measured, very small movements. Just as he came to the very end of the last beat in the bar, he would make the slightest hold and would throw several sudden darting glances in the direction of all the different sections of the orchestra. Then would follow the slightest hesitation—and down would come a fast, whipped, pile-driving, unprepared downbeat.

I have purposely used the word "unprepared" because that was exactly what it was. The downbeat was given at the last possible moment of the bar and with the shortest upbeat preparation.

This lack of a prepared accented upbeat before a big sforzando chord was typical of Toscanini. Very few other conductors do it. Normally, a conductor, even though gesticulating very discreetly, would ensure the positive attention and response of the orchestra, some of whom (such as the trombones) have not played at all before this spot, by throwing a very fast, definite upbeat just prior to the approaching chord. This upbeat, in tempo, would be a subdivided full beat, but would employ a large perpendicular movement of the arm. At the peak, it would hang in the air for a split-second pause as the orchestra synchronized itself, got itself set—and then the stroke would swiftly plummet to the next downbeat. This type of stroke telegraphs clearly to the players that the very strong downbeat chord is coming. It captures their attention and in particular prepares the woods and brass for the sharp intake of breath just before the accented downbeat. Most conductors do this; it is clear, definite, and ensures a perfect ensemble.

Toscanini's beating of this bar was somewhat different. He maintained its flavor and mood to the last possible moment, and, just as the composer intended, the final downbeat chord came as an expressive, musical, completely unexpected surprise. So, too, in his beating, he held back the surprise until the last possible moment by whipping this sudden curved upbeat.

As I have said before, Toscanini's beat made it more difficult for the orchestra to enter together. It was another example of his reliance on the players to use their own initiative. This cloaking of the "machinery" of conducting strikes at the heart of Toscanini's whole conducting manner. Even a strong climactic beat such as this, while propelled with greatest force, would actually move only a few inches. There was no theatrical pose—the beat was for us, not for the audience. Nor did he try to capitalize on the dramatic effect at our expense as if he had to exaggerate in order to make us play well. Conducting was always so instinctive with him, I doubt very much that he was aware of what he did or could have explained it.

Once the chord was played, Toscanini stood for a moment, immobile, both hands clenched close together, about waist high. Everyone seemed rooted, turned to stone. Then out shot the left hand in warning to the first violins. A sharp, flicked accent with the baton, and we were into the Allegro.

Toscanini's directions to the first violins as to how he wanted us to perform the opening bars differed on various occasions. I recall the first time we played it with him. He stopped abruptly and said, "Is no good. Is no good! The bowing—is no spirit," gesticulating with nervous, searching fingers, as though trying to feel or taste the quality he wanted. "*Vita, vita!* Dancing! Must be dancing. *Gioia!* Must be staccato." We tried again. He turned to Mischa Mischakoff, the concertmaster. "The bowing . . . I think maybe change the bowing, Mischakoff. Try—so," and he indicated with his hand a bowing stroke as though he were actually playing. "I think is good, no?"

The bowing he indicated was one seldom, if ever, used in orchestral playing. It is a stroke usually used for virtuoso effect by a solo performer. It meant slurring the two staccato notes in one up-bow after the preceding two slurred sixteenth notes of the bar. Mischakoff smiled wryly and somewhat dubiously shrugged his shoulders. "We'll try, Maestro." The men looked at one another in perplexity and somewhat patronizing disbelief. Not only had such bowing never been used here; it was not orchestral bowing in any sense at all. The men began tentatively to scrape the bows on their instruments. "Silence!" roared the Old Man, glaring murderously at the orchestra for a moment, and then, completely absorbed again, "Try together! First *violini* alone."

It was a strange, awkward bowing, a bowing, as I said, usually successfully achieved only by a first-class violinist playing alone. It would be difficult even for such a performer and almost impossible when played as a group by players of the average orchestra. But the NBC violins were "virtuoso" violins! As we played, I began to sense and grasp what the Old Man was seeking through the use of his bowing. The two staccato notes slurred in one up-bow, in conjunction with the other slurred nonstaccato down-bow notes, gave the sound a particularly lilting, skipping, dancing quality. The staccato sounded more splintery, more mercurial—it had more élan. Tap your finger several times on a piece of paper. This would illustrate the quality of a staccato—like a heavy raindrop. Now, at the same speed and same strength, instead of tapping your finger, flick the paper with finger and thumb; you will sense and hear immediately the difference in sound and in effect, although both sounds can properly be labeled "staccato."

Also, the actual manipulation of the bow had a certain rhythmic, bouncing quality; it not only sounded "dancing," it looked and felt like dancing. It imparted to the playing arm itself a skipping, dancing gesture. I sensed, through the feel, the sound, and the appearance, what it was that Toscanini was seeking in trying to replace the less sprightly usual type of bowing. The problem was one of execution—this was the snag. This kind of bowing is effective and sounds well when you play alone, but with sixteen violins, it became very difficult to achieve its intended effect. The sound became too choppy and scratchy, and the difficulty and subtlety of execution tended to blur the sharp outline of the needed ensemble. How we worked over that passage! Toscanini became angrier and angrier, goading us, sneering, "The *great* NBC first violins? Hummpff! All great soloists! Cannot play a simple *spiccato*. *Vergogna!* You are not the best—you are the worst! As soon as you have to play something outside of your stupid routine you are like children—not artists!"

There is another aspect of this bowing picture that is typical of Toscanini. In the music, there is a crescendo right from the start leading to a forte at the end of the bar and then a fortissimo at the end of the second bar. Toscanini importuned us not only to "dance" but to make a tempestuous crescendo simultaneously, demanding that it be strong and loud and at the same that *we* become vehemently dynamic in our motions, the better to achieve this stormy sound. "Use the bow! Don't sleep! *You!*" pointing in fury at a few "recalcitrant" players who did not seem frenzied enough as they bobbed about like whirling dervishes, so that the two bars of crescendo swept onward like a roaring, frothing, accumulating wave. This was difficult enough to achieve with routine bowing; with the new bowing it became almost impossible. The stroke itself is not geared for the heavy weight and excitement Toscanini demanded. It became awkward, rough, scratchy, and most uncomfortable.

With Toscanini, it must always be remembered, playing loud was not enough; it meant acting, looking loud! He demanded of us the same approach in our playing that he achieved in his conducting, except that he congealed and condensed his movements into a short space and tense motion. With us, he expected or demanded no such inhibition. When it had to sound like a frothing wave, we were truly to heave and churn like a frothing wave—spray, sand, gravel included! What physical excitement it engendered in us in spite of ourselves! We didn't just stick our toe into the bubbling waters Toscanini was stirring, we excitedly jumped in—clothes, instruments, and all! What a feeling of release and abandon! Sometimes our actual movements, our swaying bodies, bordered on the ludicrous, and the men would often smile to one another covertly (keeping a careful eye on the Old Man, however), aware of the exaggeration of the movements but caught up with the excitement. Beware the hapless player who was not giving his all, who possibly seemed slightly less involved. He would look up suddenly to see two demoniacal, blazing eyes insanely riveted on and through him! "You! *You!*" the Old Man would scream, arm and baton pointed, quivering like a harpoon ready to strike. "You! I look to *you!* Shame on you. Use the bow—*vergogna!*" The luckless player, in a paroxysm of agonized effort, would writhe madly, as though struck by a live wire. Often, the men, with a weather eye cocked in the Old Man's direction, would purposely exaggerate their movements, the better to forestall any immediate or future recrimination. But the overall effect was achieved: the drive, the spirit, the bravura were something only Toscanini managed to extract from us. Toscanini always demanded; always we gave, to the fullest measure.

We used this particular bowing, as far as I can recall, at only one or two performances. It came off well at the concerts, but because of its difficulty and roughness, it never completely gelled. I have often wondered where and how Toscanini found it.

Toscanini always liked virtuoso bowings, if possible, particularly staccato passages in one bow, as in the staccato variation in the Brahms-Haydn *Variations* and in certain Rossini overtures. He seemed to feel a particular delight in them. Perhaps it brought to mind his own effort and skill as a cellist. He would chuckle and smile as he somewhat delightedly pantomimed the ricocheting, arching motion of a flight of staccato notes with his hand while imitating the whirring sound of a machine gun, "eh-eh-eh-eh-eh-eh-eh," as he expressed to us how he wanted such notes to sound.

Many years were to pass before we were to play the *Oberon* again. A war had run its course, and only a few of the original string players were left in the first violins. I spoke to Mischakoff just before the rehearsal at which *Oberon* was scheduled. "What about the bowing, Mischa? Remember the crazy one we once played years ago with the Old Man? Should we use it now?" Mischa smiled, his eyes lighting with remembrance. "I don't know," he said somewhat dubiously. "It didn't sound so good, eh? Let's try playing

the regular bowing—maybe it will sound all right to him. I won't ask him about the other. Let's see first how it works out the regular way."

Interestingly enough, we played it the regular, orthodox way—with the excitement, of course, but without the virtuoso staccato effect. It went well, and Toscanini made no comment about the other bowing. I think he himself must have felt and heard that it was not practical, artistically tempting though it was.

This changing from performance to performance was, as I have said, very typical. One year he would, with greatest enthusiasm and fanatical conviction, insist that *this* was the right tempo, the right bowing, the right orchestration change. Another year, in the same place, he might alter or even go back to a former idea or conception, such as adding or changing a trill in the Adagio of Beethoven's Sixth Symphony, changing the orchestration at the end of the Brahms Third, changing the grace note at the opening of the *Eroica* Funeral March (bass), or completely changing the tempo, a fourth again as fast, as in the Larghetto of Beethoven's Second Symphony, saying somewhat reflectively, lips pursed, brows knit, "I think we change, eh? Yes, I think is better, no?" He would then add, in his humble, heartwarming, so earnest way, "You know, sometimes I am stupid, no? *Stupido!* An *ignorante . . .*" And, smiling: "Just like you, no?" With Toscanini, even the most familiar music seemed to pulsate reborn from rehearsal to rehearsal, from performance to performance; always there was the quality of last-moment inspiration and discovery, of something new added; always the essential purity of form and outline kept intact with uncompromising integrity; always this searching, probing, questioning. To be part of his constant reevaluation, re-creativity, was an extraordinary exhilaration.

A few words more about the opening bars of the Allegro in *Oberon*. Although marked "p," Toscanini invariably would counsel the violins not to play too softly. The two opening notes by the violins were therefore always played almost "mf." "Is never clear," the Old Man would say. "What good is to play 'piano' if nobody hear the notes? Play mezzo forte. Must be clear." We played them as if each note were accented. Sometimes, too, as we in the first violins were playing our running sixteenth-note figures, he would suddenly glower at the rest of the strings. "*Secondi violini, viole,* play staccato! Use the bow! You sleep? Play the staccato eighth notes! Play the crescendo—use bow!" He would sometimes angrily demand that they play alone. How vibrant all the plodding eighth notes became as each player suddenly bestirred himself. This accompanying eighth-note figure, normally just "played," now roared explosively, particularly in the second bar, the forte. Players who had been perfunctorily going through the motions before were suddenly staccatoing violently, their bows bouncing hysterically.

"So! So!" the Old Man would bawl passionately and derisively as he, too, plunged his baton violently in the air in a stabbing staccato motion. "So! Play!" He would glare at them; then, with a flourish of his baton to include everyone, *"To-ge-ther, TUTTI!"* We all played together. What a luminous Toscanini sound and drive filled the air, as though the size of the orchestra had been doubled.

Once this excitement was set up throughout the orchestra, we continued digging into the strings, enthusiastically using twice as much bow as was customary. The Old Man egged us on, monitoring us by stern, piercing glances, his baton, with short, potent, bouncing, clipped strokes, moving but a few inches. Four bars before Letter B, the bar of the slurred groups of eighth notes, he might call out in passing, "Separate *le note*—separate," to make sure we were not joining one group into the other. Actually, we played it as though the second note of each group had a staccato mark over it. He particularly liked this clean-cut phrasing.

When we got to B, marked "ff," Toscanini, by a warning, dampening gesture, would indicate to the woodwinds, brass, and timpani to make a special "p" immediately after the opening "ff," continuing softly and then starting a sharp crescendo on the last three eighth notes of the next bar, then again the "ff" and again the sudden "p," and so forth. Toscanini almost always used this procedure where there were large masses of harmony notes blanketing the important moving melodic passages. *"Trombone*, timpani!" he would call out violently if his gestures were not immediately grasped. "Play piano, don't play forte. *Corpo del vostro Dio!* You kill the strings. Look at me! I show you"—pointing to his stick—"no? Be quick to understand." In the second bar of B, we would dig in even harder, with special crescendo through the bar sustaining the half note.

Throughout this opening allegro, Toscanini would conduct essentially in a sharp, accented four beats to a bar. Occasionally, as the rhythm or pulse dictated—as, for example, when there were only groups of eighth notes in the bar—his beat would lapse into a pulsating subdivided alla breve in the same spirited tempo.

Four bars before Letter D, his beat would begin to slacken imperceptibly into a definite alla breve, preparing the tranquil mood of the coming clarinet solo. His grim face became calmer, his beat, up to now angular, becoming gradually more floating,

undulating downward from side to side, like a glider shifting gradually through lower air currents. His only cue to the clarinet, if there was any at all, was a characteristic raising of his eyebrows as though in warning—eyes widening, vacant and unfocused, his head inclined in the general direction of the clarinet. As the melody moved so softly along, he left the spotlight completely to the clarinet, his baton lowered almost to his waist, moving but an inch, undulating with the calm pulse of the phrasing.

Sometimes, if the clarinet seemed to be playing too loud or if the delicate accompaniment in the strings seemed to intrude, his eyes would pucker again, warningly. "Far away . . . far away . . ." he would call out in a strangled, beseeching wail. "Piano . . . piano . . . far away . . ."

The beautiful clarinet melody having softly spun its course, Toscanini would turn to the first violins, his staring eyes again widening. At rehearsals, he would often ask the first violins to play their melody alone.

"*Cantare, cantare!* Remember, play long the eighth note [the opening eighth-note upbeat] . . . *Vibrare!*"—slowly vibrating a finger over his heart. "Is a beautiful melody, no? Find the sound . . . Try . . . Is in your instrument . . . Try." With what care we placed that opening eighth note, softly, with vibrato. And still, this whole melody, in spite of the effort lavished upon it, was intoned so simply!

Beginning with the fourteenth bar after Letter D, Toscanini invariably asked for an especially exquisite bit of phrasing, a kind of phrasing only the Maestro could ask for and achieve. The tempo throughout this melody played by the first violins had been kept moving along in a straightforward manner. Beginning with the fourteenth bar, however, Toscanini imperceptibly began to broaden his alla breve beat. The bar seemed to stretch slightly; the last quarter note, the G sharp, became stickier, broader. The quarter in the next bar, the A, followed along in the same stretched manner— dragging, held back. The following downward group of sixteenth notes became even more weighted, each sixteenth, without obviously becoming slower, stretched to its widest possibility of time within the space of the beat, each note seeming to have a leaden weight under it, but still in tempo. In our parts, we actually marked dashes over each sixteenth note as a visual reminder.

Between the last note of the fourteenth bar after Letter D (the G sharp) and the following two beats ending in the sixteenth-note phrase, Toscanini also indicated a slight crescendo and diminuendo. For these two bars, he would subdivide his beat, though during the clarinet solo and melody in the first violins he had been conducting in two to the bar. "Take time, take time. Sing the small notes—graceful . . . like a *carezza*. So—so"—tenderly stroking his face with his hand. "So, play the sixteenth notes so—like a *carezza*, not like"—slapping himself in the face, and then, warming to the thought and flinging his foot in the air—"not like a kick in the—!" Then, his eyes lighting up with relish, "Understand, no? Like you caress a beautiful woman, no? You make . . . so . . ." Gently brushing his cheek. "No? Not—so!" Slapping himself violently again. "Take time on the sixteenth note—graceful—non *esagerato*. Remember—with g-o-o-d taste! Always *buon gusto*. Try!" Sometimes, in this vein, he would sing the phrase for us in a high-pitched, quavering falsetto.

All these things I have been describing were, of course, happening simultaneously. I had played this phrase countless times with different conductors, but no one made that phrase bloom so lustrously and still remain so completely in context as did Toscanini. In fact, no other conductor ever made mention of the sixteenth-note figure at all.

At Letter E, where the first violins continue with a new melody, Toscanini again did something peculiarly his own. He kept the tempo even more calm than in the preceding bars. His beat was still a sustained, subdivided alla breve. Then suddenly, at the third bar of E(83), where there is only a very slight variation of the melodic line, he changed mood and pulse almost abruptly. "Is not dreaming here, is different, now dancing, more *spirito*," he would say as his beat became tart and pointed. The whole tempo became suddenly brighter, more cheerful. I remember so clearly our surprise at this unexpected change of mood and tempo. We did not grasp immediately what he wanted; usually those four bars, starting at Letter E, were played in quite the same melodic character, with the tempo usually picking up a bit. "Is different the second time. First time is more sostenuto—the second time is different, no? More joyful. So—so"—his face lighting up, his head rocking from side to side, his baton beating four to the bar—". . . like dancing! Don't look only to your own music!"—speaking to the first violins—"Look to the score!" He lifted up the score, facing the printed page toward us. "Look! In the accompaniment to the melody. The first two bars is slow, fat, white note [whole and half notes], no? Now look to the third and fourth bars—*now* is eighth notes, rests, staccato in the accompaniment. Is different, no? Weber was not a stupid man, eh? He wanted in the second phrase a different something from the first, no? Same melody but different the accompaniment. First time tranquillo, second, dancing. Is clear, no? You understand, is in the score! I'm not stupid, no?"

Understanding better now what he meant, we played the bars with quite different emphasis. This required subtle bow manipulation, close attention to the slight, delicate pauses between the strokes that imparted the buoyant, fresher quality. We played the whole phrase again. The Old Man's face lit up with satisfaction. "*Bene! Bene!* Now is something, eh? *Molto importante* to look to the score, no? *Bene!*"

Through the next two bars, the fifth and sixth after E(85–86), Toscanini would indicate a strong continuous crescendo in the strings. He always called out to the woodwinds just before they came in at the next two bars marked "ff."

"Play forte, woodwind, play forte!" And, as though emphasizing the loudness and intensity he wanted, his head would drop suddenly, his chin taut, mouth open, shoulders tense, eyes peering balefully up at the players, his baton close to his chest, as though pushing the sound out along with them. Even during this tense pantomime, his movements were within the smallest framework. From behind him, I doubt that you could even see them. Just as the violins were ready to play the melody again (upbeat to ninth bar after E), he would brighten, once more flicking his baton in a sprightly dance tempo as he had several bars before, this time perhaps even more brightly, with the dynamics more of an "mf" rather than the "p" indicated. This continued through the four bars. Then quickly the tempo changed and again would come one of those typical Toscanini dragging rubatos. At the thirteenth bar after E(93), he would change abruptly from the lilting dance movement to a slightly broader tempo. "Sostenuto—l-o-o-ng the short notes!" he would call out. "*Cantare!* Take time on the small notes!"

Throughout the section beginning with Letter E, we had in general been very careful of the sixteenth notes of the melody. From earliest days, it had been dinned into us that, in all melodies involving notes of long and short values, we should not slight the shorter ones. In a melody such as at Letter E, we gave the two sixteenths their full melodic time value; otherwise they would become unduly hurried and lost in the overall sound pattern. This was particularly true after the broad accented quarter and dotted quarter notes in the melody. They would almost become thirty-seconds in substance and quality if one was not careful. With Toscanini, we *were* careful.

He was also adamant that grace notes be played with greatest clarity, regardless of their dynamic markings. Even when marked "p," we always gave the notes particular emphasis. When grace notes or embellishments were marked "f," Toscanini became fanatic in his demands that they be heard. Many and violent had been the scenes simply because the two grace notes (among others) in Wagner's Overture to *Tannhäuser* were not played clearly. A more heinous crime so far as Toscanini was concerned could hardly be imagined! "All over the world the same! In France—in England—in Germany—in Italy—just like in America—the same! *Asini*—nobody plays the small notes correct—never you hear the small notes!" Then, sometimes conversationally to the orchestra, "Wagner was a good conductor, not only a composer. Yes, a grand Maestro. He said in his book, 'Be careful of the small notes.'"

At the thirteenth bar after E(93), starting with the preceding two-sixteenth upbeat, the whole mood changed and became more dramatic. Toscanini gestured to us to play more turbulently, to play "mf," and not to forget to impart an accent to each dotted quarter and tied-over quarter in each bar. We also weighted and emphasized each sixteenth exaggeratedly, as though each had a separate vibrating accent over it.

Whereas for the four preceding bars (eighth bar from Letter E) Toscanini had been conducting blithely in a whipped rebounding stroke, beginning with the upbeat notes to the thirteenth bar he abruptly changed to his rolling beat. The waters were suddenly rougher, more swirling. He indicated, at the same time, bell-like accents to the half-note harmony chords in the woodwinds.

How different this sort of unexpected pesante quality was. There was a richer, more dramatic implication in the whole passage. You felt it in your hands as you played; you vibrated more feelingly on each note; your bow seemed heavier as it clung to the strings.

Six bars before F(95), we were playing almost forte, singing warmly. This forte continued for two bars, the violas and celli also imitating the expressive inner phrasing of the first violins. Then, four bars before F, Toscanini, eyes widening in signal, again changed the dynamics, which had been almost forte, to a subito mezzo piano, and in the next four bars, by gradual change of gesture, he marvelously and subtly graduated the sound, the dynamics, and the time flow back to the lighter mood and tempo. So skillfully was this done that by the time we had reached one bar before Letter F, we were already back to the original fast staccato tempo of the opening allegro.

One bar before F thus became an *a tempo* preparatory bar, so that when the bassoons and horns came in with their insistent, prancing, drumlike staccato quarter notes, it was all wonderfully joined together.

"Staccato! Short the quarters!" shrilled the Old Man in warning to those playing the accented quarters (at Letter F), using tense, nervous, firm pokes of his baton, which hardly moved. Even though it was marked "pp," there was nothing soft about how he wanted it to sound.

Toscanini insisted that the quarter notes be played more like sharp, short, accented eighth notes, as in the eighth-note accompaniment at the beginning of the Allegro. "Contrabassi!" he would suddenly bellow, pointing with shaking stick to someone in the bass section. "You! Not the *whole* bow! *Short* the bow! Like so," illustrating as though he were actually playing a bass with short, sharp strokes. There was no question,

though, that when the passage was repeated, the stroke now had the special bite that had not been there before.

Once the tempo and quality were established at F, the momentum and drive continued. *"Vita, vita,"* he would say to the first violins here, as at the beginning of the Allegro. "Remember, don't play too soft." As we got nearer to Letter G, our playing would become more and more explosive—not only louder, but with continuous, driving, broadening strokes, the celli plunging in with special excitement and release at the eighth bar before G(109).

At the sixth and fifth bars before G, everyone gave special emphasis and effort to a surging crescendo not indicated in the score, with accent on the last eighth note of the fifth bar as an upbeat to the next bar (fourth from G), roughly bouncing our bows on all of the following eighth notes, particularly the last three of the third bar before G.

It was rough, scratchy, raucous playing, unbridled in spirit, with virtuoso fervor. The Toscanini "drive"—no one else quite achieved it; no one else demanded it; no one else forced us to expend such zealous physical effort; no one else made us feel so ennobled and so personally satisfied and inspired in the process.

We charged into Letter G, woodwinds spitting out their eighth notes in bristling staccato, trombones full and resonant. In the strings, Toscanini wanted us to play the half note in the first bar as strong and long as possible, always with the smallest possible separation between it and the first of the sixteenth notes that follow. The sixteenth notes themselves were played on the G string, each note hammered in continuous crescendo at the upper half of the bow. We tried several different kinds of bowing here. Sometimes, in the heat of excitement, one way sounded particularly good, only to seem ineffectual on another occasion, but the Old Man was always willing to try a change—bowings were not sacrosanct to him.

In the second bar of G—one long, accented whole note—Toscanini demanded that we make a crescendo through the whole bar, again holding the note as long as possible, with only the *slightest* separation between it and the next note. Often such a demand was not put into actual words—it was in the air, in the tension that Toscanini maintained: his driving gesture, the stern, provocative looks he flashed in our direction, his face red with effort and tension.

How we strained in that up-bow crescendo, vibrating vigorously, attacking every note in sight with a special down-bow accent for good measure on the final quarter note in the fourth bar of G(120). Throughout this episode at G, woodwinds and trombones were brought in with gale force, with hardly a change in the driving baton stroke.

Beginning six bars before H(123), Toscanini always wanted us to play each beat accented, broad, separating each note from the other and still not playing it too short or too stiffly staccato but like a majestic march melody, with full bows and lots of vibrato.

He cautioned by eye and slight gesture—end of the eighth bar after G(124)—for the flutes and bassoons in their running scale figure to come through—not to play the "pp" indicated but a substantial "mp." This is but another instance where the resonance of the forte figure in the strings and other woodwinds playing the quarter-note melody would hang over and tend to drown out the flutes and bassoons at their entrance unless they made up for it by playing more strongly. "What good is to play 'pp' like marked if nobody hear you?"

Throughout H, too, an accented, singing quality was imparted by the instruments carrying the melody, each note broad and accented but separated. Six bars after H, the bass and celli would come crashing in with hardly any indication from the Old Man.

Four bars before Letter I(137), we in the strings would catch a sudden quiet warning movement of the stick and begin playing the quarter notes "mf," playing about half bow, separating each note and gradually increasing the amount of bow in an increasing crescendo. At this point, the celli were in the limelight, frantically digging their sixteenth notes into the strings with slashing bows and continuous crescendo.

Another typical Toscanini situation occurred two bars before Letter I. "First violins," called out the Old Man abruptly, "I don't hear you. I don't hear the beginning of the sixteenth-notes passage"—another case of short notes being covered by a preceding louder sound. "You must play louder—you are covered by the other instruments! When you play after the big sforzando, the first violins sound weak, too soft. You are alone now, no? Play *molto forte!* Take away the diminuendo in the score; play forte. I must hear the first two notes—*molto importante!*"

We went over it again, trying to play louder, accenting the opening notes with our fingers and our bows.

The Old Man dropped his arms, dissatisfied, uncertain. "Is no good. The C sharp and D [the first two notes] are not clear, must be stronger." His voice, which had started loud, became louder and more irritable. "Sixteenth notes must not sound like a subito piano, no? Is forte, no?" Turning to Mischakoff dubiously: "What bow you play?" Mischakoff played the passage. "Mischakoff! I beg you, why so many notes in one bow, why, why? Must be forte! *Brillante!*"—violently gesticulating with outstretched arms. He would sing the sixteenth-note passage several times in a loud, high-pitched voice, trying to imitate the force and passion he wanted. "So! So! I sing forte, no? Why you squeeze the notes in one bow? *Forte!* Mischakoff, please find something— change the bow!" Mischakoff tried another bowing by breaking up the passage in two strokes, permitting more bow on the first six notes. The Old Man listened, lips pursed, uncertain, unconvinced. "Yes . . . could be . . . nice . . . but the first two notes . . . must be more clear—more forte . . ."

He looked expectantly again to Mischakoff, who had in the meantime been silently trying out various bowing possibilities. "How do you like this, Maestro?"

The Old Man listened again, still uncertain. "Yes—is better, I think. We try. To-ge-ther!" The whole orchestra started back a few bars (four bars before Letter I), and again we stormed to the sforzando bar with the bowing Mischakoff had indicated. Yes, I thought, it *did* sound clearer, more forceful, the rapid moving of the changing bow strokes generating a loudness much more reverberating than before. We could feel it in the extra effort needed to encompass it. The separate strokes on the C sharp and D (starting down-bow) did give them more articulation.

At the end of the passage, the Old Man stopped again. *"Bene, bene,"* he said hesitantly. "Is good . . . but . . ." And in a wistful voice, "Is clear, yes . . ." He hesitated, groping for the right word. "If could be more accent on the two first notes, the C sharp and D, a little, little more—*appena, appena.* The separation between the long note and the first sixteenth *molto importante.*"

"Maestro," spoke up Mischakoff, "maybe this will help"—and he indicated to the violins another quite drastic change of bowing.

The Old Man brightened at the sound. "Is better, is better, I think, no? Sounds clearer the C sharp and D. *Bene.* We try—play together!" This change of bow forced the first violins to retake the bow down on the C sharp. The effort and time required to do this forced you to take more time between the sforzando note and the sixteenth. The fact that we were playing the C sharp and D at the frog of the bow added to the power and demanded even more effort and skill in its accomplishment. The awkward physical movement also added a vibrancy to the sound and to the eye. As we ripped into the passage again, the Old Man's face suddenly turned radiant. "So! So! At last I hear the small note! *Bene! Bene!* Is something now, no?" nodding his head and smiling his approval.

That good old passage, which we had played for years, hundreds of times, with so many conductors, had never seemed so significant. It was as though it had been rediscovered on Toscanini's part—and so, too, for us. We glowed with admiration and respect for the Old Man's insistence and striving for a freshness of feeling and concept that was so typically Toscanini.

Even though admitting its brilliance and clarity, not all the players were convinced about the bowing we finally used or the need for it. It was not traditional. "Rough," "exaggerated," and "unviolinistic" were the comments of some of the men; but even these diehards knew they had had an "experience"—that they had "felt" that place as they had never felt or played it before, in all its "crude" and "pagan" Toscanini splendor!

At Letter I, he would always call out, *"Cantate, oboi, cantate!"*—conducting again in sustained manner, indicating, too, that the eighth note in each bar sung by the oboes be broad, expressive. We played them as though the phrase of sixteenth notes started somewhat "mp," getting softer toward the end of the bar on the half note. His left hand was always modeling, shaping the espressivo character. "Is a melody too," he would sometimes call out. "Sing the notes; not only solfeggio."

Beginning at the fifth bar after Letter I, he would alternate his stroking—melodic singing for the woodwinds, and then short, pugnacious accents for the string figure in the next bar. Here, too, he wanted the quarter note at the beginning of the "ff" string figure to be long, bow broad, accented, with the least separation again between the quarter and eighth notes—the eighth note at the end of the bar, along with the last quarter, very square and at the same time short, indicating a crescendo that would continue unabated into K. Here again the half notes were held long, sustained, until the last moment before the accented dotted quarter, which was tied into the following eighth note, the melody always freighted with expression in spite of the pulsing march character of the accompaniment. Toscanini would always make us sustain the double dotted half note (second bar of K) in full stretched forte and then would trace a special swirling movement with his baton on the fourth beat of the bar, so that we played the last eighth note in the bar not only "correctly" but with a special emphasis on the up-bow stroke we used.

Three bars before L, he always turned to the woodwinds and horns with a sudden, "Play, *corni!* So! So! Don't play piano, play forte! Is *niente! Molto crescendo, tutti!* I speak *specialmente* to the third and fourth horn. You—don't you see me? Play forte! Play something! Don't play piano!" What a blast of sound poured forth! What had sounded rich and strong before suddenly seemed frail by comparison.

Sometimes the third and fourth horns were annoyed by Toscanini's seeming irreverence for the score. They would point to the "p" indicated (three bars before L) and grumble, "I thought Toscanini always says, 'Play what's in the score.' Well, we *are* playing what is in the score—it says 'p' and we played 'p.'" These were some of the paradoxes that often floated around. On one hand, he was exhorting you to pay attention to the score; on the other hand, he was excoriating you for *not* changing what was within. I might paraphrase his own explanation of this attitude this way:

"Don't be more royal than the king. Any *asino*, any *ignorante* can see that it says 'piano.' But what means piano? Is a thousand kinds of piano—sometimes you have to play piano louder, sometimes softer. If nobody hear you, what good is piano? There is a big crescendo in one bar, no?

"If you start too soft, too indefinite, nobody hear the first two notes in the *corni*, no? So you must play more forte to balance the whole ensemble. Music is written stupid sometimes, no? The composer writes the whole phrase piano. We must be intelligent— some instruments are low, some high, some have different *colori*. We must find the different piano in each, no? Sometime piano must be forte, sometime forte must be piano. Even if is written piano, you must be intelligent—understand something, no? Is not enough to put your nose in the score, eh? You must understand what is written, no? And anyway, you see me. I show forte with my stick, no? *Corpo del vostro Dio!*"

In Toscanini's reading of a score, he may have changed the obvious minutiae— changed the "furniture in the house" around a bit, changed some of the colors and fabrics—but he seldom if ever broke down walls, altered the foundation, or altered the inherent basic truth of the overall structure.

Back again—

With the return of the original allegro theme at L, the whole spirited playing style of the beginning was repeated until four bars before M. This entrance into M is one of the famous conductorial passages in the repertoire. Every conductor has to do something to tie these four bars effectively into the new tempo and flow at M. These four bars act as a sort of lock in a canal, bringing you up from the driving spirit and tempo to the broader, more majestic flow at M. If not done carefully, the whole passage can destroy the effectiveness of the climax. As in another famous conductorial passage, the opening of the Beethoven Fifth, every conductor does "something," including Toscanini. In this spot, to adjust this tempo for the change, Toscanini always seemed frustrated, as

though knowing what he wanted but not quite how to express it, either with words or with his hands and movements. Actually, what he asked for in outline was, as always, quite simple and logical.

Two bars before M, he began to "brake" the tempo, gradually increasing the slight ritard in a growing crescendo and intensity right until the first eighth note ("A") of the last beat of the bar before M. Then, with just the slightest hesitation and separation, he would sweep into the two unison "ff" sixteenth notes as upbeats and into the new tempo at M. This tempo at M became in the nature of an *a tempo* after the bar of the ritard immediately preceding. That was the outline; but, as with all Toscanini's outlines, it came to life with the flavor and feeling he sought only if it was played with greatest conviction and sincerest effort. This passage could not be solved by just following the musical direction of broader "f" and ritard—it required a particularly savage vehemence on our parts to make it gel. Just to "play" it made it seem watery; it needed "blood." As the Old Man often used to say when pleading with us, "Put something! Put some of your blood on the notes!"

Every time we played *Oberon*, we were sure to spend a great deal of time and effort over these few bars. The Old Man never seemed happy about them. Somehow, what he wanted or felt seemed to elude him. He whipped himself, he whipped us, into frenzied effort, but the ritard seemed too slow, too sudden—it would not flow naturally, it was not loud or triumphant enough. "Woodwinds . . . play fortissimo! Put something . . . *tutti!*" he would wail. He conducted these two bars with the greatest personal force and strength, and no matter how many times we went over them, he never spared himself.

I remember very clearly the last time we rehearsed *Oberon* with him. He was breathing heavily from exertion, dripping with perspiration. "You know," he said to the orchestra with his disarming candor and air of naïveté, "in my mind I have a picture. I remember this overture I heard played once when I was in Germany. Oh," he laughed, "was many, many years ago! Was a Czech man conducting." He wrinkled his forehead, pursed his lips. "I don't remember his name . . . but"—turning confidentially to the orchestra with great earnestness—"was a good conductor, *molto bene.*" And with approving shakes of his head, "Yes, a very good conductor! You know," he said with solemn assurance, "the Czechs are very good musicians, *si, molto bene.* This conductor conducted the same piece—it sounded wonderful! *Con spirito!* I remember, too, *how* he conducted." The Old Man beamed enthusiastically, making violent driving motions, as though describing the movements of the conductor. "Yes! Was a good conductor, but"—he shook his head sadly—"all these years I conducted this piece, I try to do what he did, to make it sound that way, but *strano* (strange), is never good. Something is missing—something. I don't know why . . . I try. . ." He shrugged his shoulders sadly, and then, with renewed conviction: "*Andiamo!* We try again . . . Remember . . . *poco ritardo . . . molto forte* . . . Look at me! Try!"

At one rehearsal, the Old Man suggested perhaps the violas in octaves should double the woodwinds the greater support and sonority. This we used once, discarded later. At the last rehearsal, however, the Old Man suggested something that seemed quite bizarre and strange for him. He asked us to put a much longer wait between the last eighth note and the two sixteenth notes before M. All along we had been putting a very slight separation there; now, however, he was indicating a much larger separation, almost as long as an eighth note in length. This put a hole between these notes, so that one phrase ended very definitely before another began. Whereas before the final beat before M had always been accomplished with a combination of an accent and a wide flourish of the baton that encompassed the slight separation, now he wanted a definite stop and gave another stroke of the baton for the sixteenths. It seemed very exaggerated in sound—awkward for him to conduct and for us to execute. However, he insisted, and at the last performance we played *Oberon* with him, that was the way we did it.

We continued through M with great gusto, always with the admonition, "The small notes [sixteenths], forte the small notes!" ringing in our ears. Every note was very heavily accented within the bar, with special emphasis on the *first* of the two sixteenths to make sure they were heard. It was very exaggerated in motion but gave great clearness to the sixteenth, which ordinarily would have been blurred. In the accompaniment, too, Toscanini asked for great effort so that it all sounded like one long, vibrant drumroll, everyone playing the eighth note very staccato, particularly the violas, celli, and basses, who used this bowing to very good effect. Toscanini invariably liked to have us use a bowing that normally would seem awkward, unviolinistic. But it was this very awkwardness that, in its process of execution of motion, forced us to work harder, imparting that particular "flavor" of intensity and fervor to a phrase—a fervor it would not have had had it been played in a routine, legitimate manner.

For Toscanini, it was never enough to hear that the music was loud; he had to feel and see the effort that went into the process. This power and resonance he sought so constantly could not be achieved by any other approach. You had to get out and shovel; you had to sweat!

Here ends the manuscript.

Sam coming offstage after conducting a New Jersey Symphony concert.

CODA

MY FATHER'S BOOK ENDS as abruptly as his life. He passed away before he could create a closing chapter. The publisher added the words, "Here ends the manuscript," leaving us to wonder what more Dad would have shared with his readers.

Perhaps he was saving the best for last. In my search through his papers, I found a few handwritten lines to suggest how Dad might have concluded his story of the Maestro and of his seventeen years with the NBC Symphony. He wrote:

> *Years of tumultuous memories continued until that tragic day when he announced his retirement after a harrowing concert in April 1954. As our beloved eighty-seven-year-old Maestro left the stage, dazed and tottering, he pushed past me, and the baton dropped from his hand. It was to be the last of his conducting in public.*
>
> *No more to hear the hoarse, frenzied, "Vergogna!" balefully rending the air. No more to hear the menacing, "Corpo del vostro Dio!"*
>
> *I had "played with Toscanini"—the musician's supreme badge of honor. I knew that music performed with sacrificial white heat, passion, humility, and blinding honesty can be unforgettable.*

My father died in January 1958, at forty-nine—almost a year to the day after Arturo Toscanini's death, in January 1957, at age eighty-nine. It was an ordinary winter afternoon in between concert engagements. Dad was walking briskly across West Fifty-Seventh Street, already late for a luncheon meeting with his manager, when, just a few doors away from Carnegie Hall, he fell to the sidewalk, struck down by a fatal heart attack. As the police told my mother when they came to her door an hour later, he could not be revived. In minutes, the beloved and charismatic force in our lives was gone. A flourishing career cut short.

How did this happen? Had he felt ill that morning when he called out, "See you later," as I rushed out the door for school? Was his schedule too strenuous? He was certainly in demand, thriving on all the opportunities that came his way. He had recently returned home from a concert in Houston, and only a couple of months earlier he had been hailed in his hometown of Chicago as the new assistant conductor to Fritz Reiner, the music director of the Chicago Symphony. That appointment had not only given Dad a burst of professional pride but also struck a deep personal chord. His whole Chicago family showed up for each of those November concerts, thrilled to see their precious "Sammy" on the podium receiving ovations from his admiring audiences.

With my father's sudden death, the music world had surely lost a rising star, but I had lost my hero, my protector, and my loving Daddy, who beat 4/4 time with his baton while I practiced the piano and who held my hand tightly when he walked me to school. I had lost the enthusiastic conductor I loved to watch bounce up and down on his toes to the pulsing rhythm of Bizet's "March of the Toreadors." I still hold that image dear to my heart.

My mother's grief was profound; her numbing sorrow seemed to be limitless. Dad had been her first and now would be her last true love. Overnight she went from being a wife, muse, partner, and half of a royal musical couple to a widow facing a dwindling bank account and a young daughter to raise on her own.

Letters, phone calls, and moving tributes poured in. As friends and family came to pay their respects, I watched silently from the sidelines, not sure how to behave or what to say, afraid that my mother might disappear as suddenly as my father had. Mom rose to the occasion with her usual grace and inner strength, but all the expressions of sympathy, all the awards and scholarships soon established in his name, all the kind words could not alter or ease the fact that our little family had been upended. "Three" had now become "two." We were on our own.

Mom never tired of reminding me how alike he and I were, and I never tired of hearing about it. "Your eyes crinkle up just like his when you smile." They do? "He tilted his head to the side the same way you do when listening to music." He did? "Your hands look just like his." Yes, I guess they do. I found comfort in those small discoveries. I don't recall ever hearing, "You have the same frown or bad temper as your dad." He must have had some moody moments, but his dying so young pushed all criticism into the background.

I know I resemble him more than I do my mother. Like me, he was tall. He also had hazel eyes and a light complexion. Staying in the sun a minute too long turned us both beet red. Red hair was prevalent in his family, but neither my father nor I had flaming crimson locks—just a hint of henna peeking through. He was great at telling jokes—his timing impeccable—but I didn't inherit that trait. I mangle the punch line every time. I am musical but not a musician. I can sing on key and have a good "ear," and I may get teary when I hear Itzhak Perlman play Tchaikovsky's Violin Concerto in D Major or when Pavarotti hits one of his high Cs, but I never studied music after my early years of piano lessons.

My parents encouraged me to pursue all my interests and ever-changing passions. I can hear their words so clearly. "Don't be afraid of change. Try new things, and find what you love." And that is what I've done.

I inherited my mother's gift for creating art and had a pencil in my hand from age four. Mom and I would sit together in Riverside Park, sketchpad and charcoal stick at the ready. She'd point to a tree, or a pigeon, or the Good Humor ice cream truck and say, "Draw what you see," never pressuring and always making it fun.

When I became hooked on ballet, I studied with lofty ambitions, dreaming of pirouetting *en pointe* in a sequined tutu. But once I entered New York's famed High School of Music and Art—majoring in art—I put my toe shoes away, let my hair out of the requisite dancer's bun, and got busy with my paints and brushes.

To my mother's surprise, I did not choose music, dance, or art as my career. I went in another direction—away from center stage. I was drawn to the intriguing backstage world of television production. I wanted to become part of the team that created and shaped the programming. I wanted to be in the room where the big decisions were made. What scenes to cut? What joke needed a rewrite? Do we need to recast that part? I also wanted to see my name roll by on the closing production credits. All of which I eventually achieved.

However, my first job was hardly glamorous. As a clerk typist in the record library at NBC, I earned seventy-five dollars a week cataloguing the dozens of new LPs that arrived each day, adding to the already vast album collection. It might have been a lowly entry position, but as far as I was concerned, I was officially in show business!

Each morning when I passed through the revolving doors of the majestic RCA Building at "30 Rock" and strode past the huge wall murals, my high heels clicking on the marble floor, I felt a sense of empowerment as I headed to the NBC studio elevators—the same elevators that Toscanini and my father had taken to reach Studio 8H in the 1940s and 1950s. Dad and I had come full circle.

After many decades in the entertainment industry, working my way up from assistant to the assistant to the producer to a network senior vice presidency, there was no doubt I had made the right choices. I often look up and give a silent thank-you to my parents for giving me the courage and foundation to follow my own path.

Soon after Dad died, Mom had to rapidly reinvent herself. She sharpened her artistic skills and developed a specialty: teaching the finer points of freehand sketching to interior designers. Her course became so popular that she gave yearly seminars in New York and London. I can just hear her saying, "Who would have thought?"

It took more than a year before Mom could even consider the idea of preparing Dad's manuscript for publication. The loss was still too raw for her. "How am I possibly going to do this?" she'd wail. "These pages belong to him!" She had been at his side from the beginning, inspiring him, helping him edit and polish all his drafts, but there was so much more work to do. With the support of friend and publisher Evelyn Shrifte, Mom began to face the daunting task of completing the project. She was determined that Dad's life's work—our legacy—have the impact he had intended. When she was asked to write a closing chapter, she refused, insisting that the book be published just as he wrote it. "Let it all be in his words," she said.

From 1960 to 1963, preparing the manuscript was a consuming endeavor. Along with fine-tuning some of Dad's text, Mom had to choose the photographs that would appear in the book. Some would be culled from the NBC archives, many from our own collection, and others came from fellow musicians. But the featured photographs—the ones which have become iconic portraits of the Maestro—were taken by Robert Hupka, then an RCA recording engineer. During the mid-1940s, Hupka had candidly captured Toscanini's many expressive moods during rehearsals, performances, and recording sessions.

A few nights every week, Mom and Robert sat at our dining room table, hunched over piles of his exquisite photos, sorting through the hundreds of choices, selecting just the right ones to illustrate particular sections of my father's manuscript. The result, as we now know, was a magnificent combination of art forms—each creator enhancing the other's work.

This Was Toscanini was published in November 1963, garnering lavish praise. It continues to be a hallmark for written works about the Maestro's remarkable approach to music. In his *New York Times* review, Edward Downes stated: "This book will probably remain the most enduring and endearing monument to the art of Arturo Toscanini." And it has.

Through the process of compiling this new edition, researching and writing all the new material about Dad, and about us, he and I have joyfully been brought back together, creating our own duet and forming a longed-for and much belated relationship. We may have had only twelve years together, and I may not have had him to guide me through my rocky teenage years, but his influence and his powerful presence are deeply ingrained in who I am. There will forever be an invisible thread connecting us. Thanks to this journey of rediscovery, I can embrace who he was from an adult perspective rather than from the limited memory of an adoring young daughter.

Only now, after spending so much time looking through photos, reading his letters, hearing his voice on radio broadcasts, listening to old recordings of his exquisite violin playing, and yelling, "There he is!" when I catch a glimpse of him on a YouTube clip, am I able to say goodbye to him with a light heart.

Who was Samuel Antek? He was a man of abundant talents, intense passions, infectious personality, and powerful discipline. He was a sensual, curious, stimulating man, filled with innovative creative dreams. He was a leader in every path he pursued, never straying from his original dream—a life filled with music. He was my Dad.

And what of Arturo Toscanini? As I worked on this new edition, the Maestro made a deep personal impression on me. Reading my father's words, I developed an unexpected soft spot for the "Old Man." He was no longer just the imposing figure in the photo on top of our piano or the one making timeless music on our radio. He was a man of many colorful dimensions whom I grew to respect, honor, and, yes, enjoy—outrageous outbursts and all. This irascible, brilliant, politically courageous, privately shy force of nature was someone I'd have loved to have known.

George Szell, eminent conductor of the Cleveland Orchestra, put it best when he said, "Toscanini was a truth seeker. . . . There was before Toscanini and after Toscanini."

And thus ends *my* manuscript, a tribute to two musicians whose paths fortuitously crossed and whose individual gifts inspired each of them in their lifelong quest to make beautiful music.

ACKNOWLEDGMENTS

TWO SUMMERS AGO, JUST as I was pondering how to approach the reissue of this book, a pair of finches landed on the sill just outside my office window. They returned each day, appearing to stare at me as I tapped away on the computer. They'd peck at the windowpane, flutter their wings, then abruptly fly away. This went on for a few weeks.

Clearly—at least to me—their visits were a sign from above. I was sure they were bringing me a message from my parents, who were granting me a thumbs-up, infusing me with the confidence I needed to move forward with my labor of love.

Guess what? I subsequently discovered that the finches weren't looking at me after all. They were, in fact, drawn to the windowpane by their own reflections in the glass when the sun was at a certain angle—usually around noon. Whatever the reason—whether pure nature or divine intervention—it worked! Here I am at the conclusion of this exhilarating and liberating journey, eager to give special thanks to those who played a significant role in shaping this project and making my "What if?" into a reality.

One of the singular pleasures on this adventure has been getting to know Harvey Sachs. I first contacted him in 2017 after reading David Denby's glowing review of Harvey's Toscanini biography in the *New Yorker*. I wanted to congratulate him and thank him for featuring some portions of my father's narrative in his new book. Those were the sparks that ignited the idea to reissue *This Was Toscanini*.

After rounds of emails, Harvey and I finally met in person one wet January afternoon at an Upper West Side bistro. Not only did he think I was on a worthy quest, but he asked the most generous question: "How can I be of help?" His enthusiasm and ongoing support have been invaluable. Thank you, Harvey.

My next stop was to see friend and attorney Alan Neigher, who deftly guided me through the legal and practical issues I would encounter. Fortunately, I was able to unearth old files that had been tucked away in storage for thirty years. They were filled with book contracts and publisher correspondence from the 1950s through the 1980s, offering a clear road map of the original book's history. Alan encouraged me to add fresh material to this new edition, though at that point I had no idea what I would include or how to take the first step.

It was on a visit with my close friend Judy Nichtern and her son Matthew Bird—both artists, designers, and writers—that my mission crystallized. Once they expressed the very simple statement, "We want to know more about your father," all the pieces clicked into place. I realized that I could not only preserve my father's work but, through my own memories and personal memorabilia, bring his life and legacy into focus.

A practiced writer I am not, but I had two inspiring teachers along the way. Thanks to longtime friend and writer Linda Schreyer—who had been my upstairs neighbor during our growing-up years in New York and was then my neighbor in Los Angeles—I was introduced to the wonders of memoir writing. In her weekly workshops, as I drew upon my own history as a basis for storytelling, I became hooked on this personal form of expression.

When we moved back east to Westport, I joined a memoir writing group. This kept me brimming with ideas, but it wasn't until I connected with Mary-Lou Weisman—accomplished writer, journalist, inspiring teacher, and, best of all, friend—that I became more serious about my commitment to memoir writing. Through her insightful instruction, my nonstop writing (and rewriting!), and our hours of conversation about this project, I more fully developed the framework and confidence for how to turn a personal anecdote into a structured story.

A particular thank-you to dear friend Susan Pollock. As a television and film producer with strong connections in publishing, she gave me the best gift of all: she introduced me to editor Jo Ann Miller. "She will make all the difference—you'll see." And that she has. Jo Ann's taste, experience, and gentle nudges to delve even deeper into personal territory *did* make all the difference in shaping my new essays. Thank you, Jo Ann.

A loving thank-you to my cousins Toby Falk, Rick Komar, and Susan Rothschild, who eagerly shared stories about their beloved "Uncle Sam," helping me form a clearer picture of my father's life—and my own early years.

I am particularly grateful to Arthur Fierro, the executor of photographer Robert Hupka's estate. His devotion to the material, along with his diligence, perseverance, and exhaustive research, provided me with access to Hupka's precious original photos, which were central to closing the circle on this book.

In the early days of 2020, I was introduced to literary agent Coleen O'Shea. Her belief in my project became a beam of hope during that upside-down year of pandemic lockdown. Through emails, video conferences, and lengthy phone calls, she expertly guided me through the mystifying (to me) world of publishing—an ever-evolving industry I knew little about—and ultimately found the right home for me at Brown Books. Thank you, Coleen, and thank you to Tom Reale and the dedicated Brown Books Publishing team: Alex Charest, Hallie Raymond, and Samantha Williams, who all, with their special skills, helped me realize my dream.

Many years ago, I donated boxes of my father's correspondence, photographs, and other professional memorabilia to the New York Public Library of the Performing Arts at Lincoln Center—a revered reservoir of arts research material. I could not have predicted that one day I would be spending hours in their hushed and carefully guarded reading room, diving into the Antek archives and reacquainting myself with Dad's musical history. Every few months, I returned to reread a letter, discover another article, or review the abundant and familiar photographs. Time well spent. Although I had duplicate copies of many of these pieces in my own files, sitting in that quiet room and slowly absorbing the material gave me the clarity and inspiration I needed to stay on course.

When I first met Meryl Moss, I hoped that we would one day work together—all I needed was a publishing deal and a release date! Well, here we are, a couple of years later, at last joined in a mutual effort to introduce this book to a new audience. Thank you to the Meryl Moss Media and BookTrib teams.

And I especially want to give recognition to those friends and colleagues who each contributed a unique ingredient to this work—whether it was asking a probing question, offering an added memory or a welcome critical comment, introducing me to a helpful new resource, or helping me navigate track changes on the computer for the umpteenth time. Thank you, Joan Cowlan, Nancy Dussault, Marcia Falk, Sonny Fox, David Garrison, John Gillan, Barbara Meltzer, Karen Morrow, Maggie Mudd, Beverly and Harvey Newmark, Marco Pavia, Cynthia Raymond, Jay Shulman, Sybil Steinberg, Susan Tane, Karen and Barry Tarshis, Larry Weisman, and Rita Weisskoff.

And the biggest thank-you of all to my most precious partner, Bill Klein—my number-one cheerleader, patient proofreader, critic, advisor, and all-around best husband ever!

PHOTO CREDITS

Robert Hupka

The candid photographs of Arturo Toscanini by Robert Hupka on the front cover, the back cover, and pages xiv, 7, 10, 14, 17, 22, 27, 33, 38, 43, 53, 76, 81, 119, 125, 129, 133, 136, 142, 149, and 153 were taken during many NBC Symphony rehearsals, broadcasts, and recording sessions—without the Maestro's knowledge.

Photographer Robert E. Hupka was born and raised in Vienna and emigrated to the United States at the onset of World War II in order to escape Nazi persecution. His love of music and technical skills landed him a position with RCA Victor as director of their record library, offering him access to his musical idol, Arturo Toscanini. His now iconic black-and-white portraits, first introduced in the original edition of *This Was Toscanini*, have since been featured on album covers and in exhibitions around the world.

A cameraman and audio technician for CBS Television for forty years, Hupka also received international acclaim for his photographs of Michelangelo's *Pietà*, taken while it was on view in the Vatican Pavilion at the 1964 New York World's Fair. Hupka died in 2001, leaving an exceptional photographic legacy.

Additional Photo Credits

Irving Chidnoff xx

Jacques Larner xxviii

Samuel Antek 47, 50, 51, 54

Sy Friedman, National Broadcasting Company 59, 63, 65, 72, 90

New Jersey Symphony 84, 87

Herbert Lehr, *Life* 94

Emerich Gara 161

James Abresch 169

Elizabeth Tapia 171

All other images are courtesy of the author.

SAMUEL ANTEK

Samuel Antek began his violin studies in Chicago and was then invited to New York to become a pupil and protégé of the famous teacher Leopold Auer. He soon won a fellowship to attend the Juilliard Foundation and, following his New York debut at Town Hall, played solo concerts extensively. In 1937, Mr. Antek was selected to become a first violinist for the NBC Symphony, an orchestra specially created by RCA for the legendary conductor Arturo Toscanini. He was a member of the orchestra for all of its seventeen years, from 1937 to 1954.

With the support and encouragement of the Maestro and the guidance of conductor Pierre Monteux, Antek was able to launch his own career as a conductor. While continuing to play first violin for NBC, he was appointed musical director and conductor of the New Jersey Symphony in 1947; was named the associate conductor of the Chicago Symphony under Fritz Reiner; and, after inaugurating his distinctive

Young People's Concerts series in New Jersey, was soon named the director of all Young People's Concerts of the Philadelphia Orchestra. He was invited to guest conduct many of the nation's major orchestras, including the NBC Symphony, Houston Symphony, and Buffalo Philharmonic, among others.

Samuel Antek died suddenly at age forty-nine in January 1958. *This Was Toscanini*, his unique evaluation of the Maestro, was published posthumously.

LUCY ANTEK JOHNSON

Lucy Antek Johnson, Samuel Antek's daughter, was born and raised in New York City. After studying music, fine art, and ballet, she was drawn to the world of television production and spent her entire career in the entertainment industry, working with such producers as Martin Charnin, Harry Belafonte, David Susskind, and Roone Arledge. When she moved to Los Angeles in 1978, she produced movies for television, then joined the ranks of NBC as a network executive. She soon worked her way up to senior vice president of daytime and children's programs for CBS, a position she held for fourteen years.

Lucy and her husband, Bill Klein, live in Connecticut, where she has served on the Westport Library's board of trustees and continues to work with the library on special programming projects. She paints, writes, and—every so often—gets up the nerve to sit at the piano and play a favorite Bach or Chopin prelude.